Presented to

_____

By

_____

On the Occasion of

_____

Date

_____

Peace
LIKE A RIVER

DEVOTIONAL THOUGHTS OF COMFORT
FROM CLASSIC CHRISTIAN HYMNS

DANIEL PARTNER

BARBOUR
PUBLISHING, INC.
Uhrichsville, Ohio

Peace
LIKE A RIVER

DEVOTIONAL THOUGHTS OF COMFORT
FROM CLASSIC CHRISTIAN HYMNS

Published by Barbour Publishing, Inc., P.O. Box 719, Uhrichsville, Ohio 44683 http://www.barbourbooks.com

ecpa Member of the
Evangelical Christian
Publishers Association

Printed in the United States of America.

CONTENTS

INTRODUCTION

Like a river glorious is God's perfect peace,
Over all victorious in its bright increase;
Perfect, yet it floweth fuller every day,
Perfect, yet it groweth deeper all the way.

FRANCES R. HAVERGAL[1]

In the beginning, when paradise could still be found on earth, there was a river whose fountainhead watered the garden in Eden (Genesis 2:10). Those who dwelt in that garden ate of the tree of life and walked with God among the trees while they drank water from this river of God's pleasures (Psalm 36:8). As the hymnist Haldor Lillenas[2] describes, they had "peace like a river, so deep and so broad. . ."

Wonderful peace, wonderful peace;
Resting my soul on the bosom of God,
I have peace, sweet peace.

Genesis tells that the river watered the whole earth by dividing into four as it flowed out of the garden. One of these rivers was called the Tigris; another was the Euphrates. The ages passed. Eventually a time came when people sat by these same rivers in Babylon. They sat there and they wept (Psalm 137:1). Why? Simply put, they were hopelessly separated from God. They then knew that God's words were true: "If only you had paid attention to my commands, your peace would have been like a river, your righteousness like the waves of the sea" (Isaiah 48:18 NIV).

Though it was replaced by a river of tears in the human soul, the river of God did not dry up. This is why an ancient Hebrew poet could declare, "There is a river whose streams make glad the city of God" (Psalm 46:4 NIV), and God would say, "Rejoice with Jerusalem and be glad for her, all you who love her. . .[because] I will extend peace to her like a river" (Isaiah 66:10, 12 NIV).

Later, God did impart peace by visiting the earth as a man, watering and enriching the earth with the river of God (see Psalm 65:9).

He was Jesus Christ, who stood in the Temple of Jerusalem and shouted to the crowds, "If you are thirsty, come to me! If you believe in me, come and drink! For the Scriptures declare that rivers of living water will flow out from within" (John 7:37–38 NLT).

This book is a collection of the lyrics to forty hymns about God's comfort in suffering. Each is accompanied by a few paragraphs that tell my thoughts and meditations about its meaning. But this book is not about hymns. It is about being thirsty enough to believe in Jesus Christ and drink of the river of God's pleasures.

Thirst is suffering and suffering is a kind of thirst, so God's comfort flows in the river of water of life. American slaves were thirsty enough to drink from this river. This is why, as they labored they sang,

> *I've got peace like a river,*
> *I've got peace like a river,*
> *I've got peace like a river in my soul.*

Someday the earth will dissolve and vanish (2 Peter 3:10–11). Then a new heaven and a new earth will appear with the new Jerusalem at its center. God will live among us and there will be no more suffering—no death or sorrow or crying or pain (see Revelation 21:1–4). And the river of water of life, the very river that began its flow in the paradise of long ago, will continue to flow clear and bright as crystal (22:1). Then, as Isaac Watts[3] once sang,

The saints shall flourish in his days,
Dressed in the robes of joy and praise;
Peace, like a river from his throne,
Shall flow to nations yet unknown.

DANIEL PARTNER
Sisters, Oregon
June 2001

NOTES

[1] Frances R. Havergal (1836-1879) was a British hymn writer. Other hymns of hers are found on pages 132 and 137.

[2] Haldor Lillenas (1885-1959) was an American evangelist and pastor who wrote some four thousand hymns.

[3] Isaac Watts (1674-1748), the British hymn writer who wrote "Joy to the World," revolutionized church music with his original compositions.

A Little Bird I Am

A little bird I am,
Shut from the fields of air,
And in my cage I sit and sing
To him who placed me there;
Well-pleased a prisoner to be,
Because, my God, it pleaseth thee.

Nought have I else to do,
I sing the whole day long;
And he whom most I love to please
Doth listen to my song;
He caught and bound my wandering wing;
But still he bends to hear me sing.

Thou hast an ear to hear,
A heart to love and bless;
And though my notes were e'er so rude,
Thou wouldst not hear the less;
Because thou knowest as they fall,
That love, sweet love, inspires them all.

My cage confines me round;
Abroad I cannot fly;
But though my wing is closely bound,
My heart's at liberty;
For prison walls cannot control
The flight, the freedom of the soul.

O it is good to soar
These bolts and bars above!
To him whose purpose I adore,
Whose providence I love;
And in thy mighty will to find
The joy, the freedom of the mind.

JEANNE GUYON (1648–1717)

French aristocrat Madame Jeanne Guyon was a widow and the mother of grown children when she was imprisoned in the Bastille, the infamous prison in Paris. The eight stone towers of the formidable fortress, each measuring one hundred feet tall, that dominated the cityscape of Paris for four hundred years were linked to each other by walls of equal height. To complete the picture, the Bastille was surrounded by a moat more than eighty feet wide.

At age fifty Jeanne Guyon was locked in a prison cell for four years. There, in the Bastille, she wrote the words to this hymn.

But the Bastille was not Jeanne Guyon's first jail. As a young woman she had entered into an arranged marriage with a man who was twenty-two years her senior. Though Jeanne was a good and faithful helpmate to her husband, her mother-in-law tried to make her life miserable. She preferred the household servants to her son's beautiful wife, concocted arguments when Jeanne expressed her opinions, and fed her son false stories about his wife. Yes, Madame Guyon's original prison was her family.

We may find some connection with Madame Guyon by asking this question: What is a prison? Certainly it is a place of severe limitation and punishment. But we are often so limited in our families, our jobs, our finances, and our bodies that these seem to be prisons from which there is no escape. But are they God's punishment for our misdeeds? Absolutely not!

When Jeanne Guyon was restricted by her mother-in-law, she turned to prayer. She understood that just as God had made Joseph a slave in Egypt, so she was placed in a household with such a mother-in-law, and, as it was with Joseph, "God meant it unto good" (Genesis 50:20 KJV).

Besides the psychological trauma of her home life, Madame Guyon experienced physical tragedies as well. As a young woman, her beauty was marred by smallpox—the disease that took the life of her eldest son—and she was widowed with three children at age twenty-eight. But by then she had laid hold of two central principles that can rule one's moral life. One makes man the center of life and the other makes God life's center. Guyon lived by the latter principle— God was her center.

For eight years Madame Guyon traveled throughout France and Switzerland as an apostle of the Quietist movement, teaching that spiritual perfection is attained when self is lost in the contemplation of God. But church leaders were jealous of her popularity with the common folk. At about the time Guyon became influential in the French royal court, the church began to persecute Christian mystics. She was falsely charged with heresy, her books were publicly burned, her mail seized, and her property vandalized. In 1798 she was imprisoned at the Bastille.

Madame Guyon believed that as gravity is to the physical world, faith is to the spiritual world. Thus, faith has the power to make one's heart holy—sanctified from selfishness. Such a heart is enabled to love God with all its power (see Mark 12:30).

PRAYER

Dear heavenly Father, may I myself no longer live, but let Christ live in me. I want to live my life on this earth by trusting in the Son of God, who loved me and gave himself for me.

ALL IN HIS HANDS

"All in his hands"—what confidence it brings
To tested hearts, to know that all the things
That make up life and circumstance, he holds
In his strong hands, and patiently unfolds
Th' eternal purpose of his sovereign will—
That all things shall his grace and glory fill.

"All in his hands"? Then life with purpose moves
Within the circle of his will, and proves
It good, acceptable. The hands of man
Or Satan cannot mar or foil the plan
Which God ordained—to manifest his Son
In earthen vessels, to a world undone.

K. O. McNair

This hymn contains an important message hidden within its old poetic style. Although this style uses words in a beautiful way, it can sometimes obscure their meaning, especially for the modern reader. Here is what the first verse says without the ornate poetics:

> *Everything is in God's hands, that is,*
> *under God's control. When people who are*
> *being tested in the circumstances of life*
> *understand this, they find strength and*
> *courage to pass through their suffering.*
> *Why? Because they know that God*
> *patiently unfolds the eternal purpose even*
> *in their lives. In the end all things will be*
> *filled with divine grace and glory.*

Now recall the familiar words of Romans 8:28: "And we know that in all things God works for the good of those who love him, who have been called according to his purpose" (NIV). Do you see how this verse echoes the idea expressed in the hymn?

Recently I saw the reality of this hymn in my son's life. He was failing some important courses in high school and he ran into trouble with the police in our little town. My son badly needed a fresh start and so my wife and I sent him to live with some folks who have a small ranch a couple of hours away. There, in a Christian family setting, he lived and worked in a very structured environment. Prayers were answered and over a couple of months my son came to some vital realizations about how he should live his life.

He has seen that I am not living in his family, but that he is living in mine. This simple fact is a key to Romans 8:28. You did not invite God to be a part of your life's purpose. Rather, God has an eternal purpose and has included you in it. All the things that happen to you work to fulfill God's purpose and are good for you.

Romans 8:29 gives an outline of the eternal purpose of God: "For those God foreknew he also predestined to be conformed to the likeness of his Son, that he might be the firstborn among many brothers" NIV. God's purpose for your life and for mine is the same for every believer in Christ—to be conformed to the likeness of the Son, or to become like Jesus Christ.

This brings us to verse two of the hymn.

Again, here it is in unadorned form:

> *Is everything in life under God's con-*
> *trol? When one answers "Yes" to this ques-*
> *tion, then that person's life moves with*
> *purpose within the circle of God's will.*
> *Such a life proves that God's will is good,*
> *and acceptable, and perfect (Romans*
> *12:2). The effort of man or Satan cannot*
> *ruin or defeat the plan which God estab-*
> *lished—to let the ruined world clearly see*
> *Jesus Christ in fallen and redeemed*
> *humanity (2 Corinthians 4:6, 7).*

MEDITATION

For God, who commanded the light to
shine out of darkness, hath shined in our
hearts, to give the light of the knowledge
of the glory of God in the face of Jesus
Christ. But we have this treasure in
earthen vessels, that the excellency of the
power may be of God, and not of us. We
are troubled on every side, yet not distressed;

*we are perplexed, but not in despair; per-
secuted, but not forsaken; cast down, but
not destroyed; always bearing about in the
body the dying of the Lord Jesus, that the
life also of Jesus might be made manifest
in our body (2 Corinthians 4:6–10 KJV).*

ALL THE WAY
MY SAVIOR LEADS ME

All the way my Savior leads me;
What have I to ask beside?
Can I doubt his tender mercy,
Who through life has been my guide?
Heav'nly peace, divinest comfort,
Here by faith in him to dwell!
For I know, whate'er befall me,
Jesus doeth all things well;
For I know, whate'er befall me,
Jesus doeth all things well.

All the way my Savior leads me,
Cheers each winding path I tread,
Gives me grace for every trial,
Feeds me with the living bread.
Though my weary steps may falter,
And my soul athirst may be,
Gushing from the rock before me,
Lo! A spring of joy I see;

Gushing from the rock before me,
Lo! A spring of joy I see.

All the way my Savior leads me;
O the fullness of his love!
Perfect rest to me is promised
In my Father's house above.
When my spirit, clothed immortal,
Wings its flight to realms of day,
This my song through endless ages:
Jesus led me all the way;
This my song through endless ages:
Jesus led me all the way.

FANNY CROSBY (1820–1915)

When the people of Israel fled from Egypt and into the wilderness, the leading of God was hard to miss. Indeed, the Bible says that the Lord guided them by a pillar of cloud during the day and a pillar of fire at night (see Exodus 13:21). It goes without saying that we live in different times. Although as believers we are still on a journey with God, we aren't led along the way by outward signs. After all, Christ dwells in our hearts by faith (see Ephesians 3:17).

When the apostle Paul recalled the journey of Israel, he wrote, "I don't want you to forget, dear brothers and sisters, what happened to our ancestors in the wilderness long ago. God guided all of them by sending a cloud that moved along ahead of them. . . ." (1 Corinthians 10: 1 NLT). Despite this cloud, the Israelites were often fearful. In Exodus 17 the people came to a place in the desert called Rephidim. There was no water to be found there so they complained to Moses, "Give us water to drink!" They were sorry they had ever embarked on their journey with God and thought they all would surely die (vv. 1–3 NLT).

Although they were traveling with a fantastical, miraculous, visible leader—the cloud of fire—they were not comforted. Despite the presence of the pillar of cloud, which was most likely the Lord, the Israelites were afraid they would fail and never reach their destination. Have you ever felt this way about your journey with God?

Moses was at a loss: "What should I do with these people?" he cried to God. "They are about to stone me!" (v. 4 NLT). The Lord replied, "Take your shepherd's staff. . .and walk on ahead of the people. I will meet you by the rock at Mount Sinai. Strike the rock, and water will come pouring out. Then the people will be able to drink" (see vv. 5–6). Moses did as he was told and sure enough, water gushed out of the rock.

Later, as Israel wandered through the wilderness, they always knew that God was their rock (see Psalm 78:35), their new companion on the long journey. As Paul wrote, "All drank the same spiritual drink. For they drank from the spiritual rock that followed them, and the rock was Christ" (1 Corinthians 10:4 NRSV).

The gospel tells the story of this Rock of Ages. When Jesus hung on the cross, one of his guards committed a final act of cruelty and pierced his side with a spear. Blood and water flowed out (see John 19:33–34). I am unspeakably grateful for this because now I can drink from the rock who is Jesus Christ. And so can you.

Christ the rock travels with us on the way of faith. The leading of God is this refreshing person. We are not led in the old, visible, miraculous way since we walk by faith and not by sight (see 2 Corinthians 5:7). We are led along by the flowing refreshment of the water of life. "Let the one who believes in me drink," said Jesus. "As the scripture has said, 'Out of his belly shall flow rivers of living water'" (John 7:38 KJV).

MEDITATION

For the Lamb at the center of the throne will be their shepherd; he will lead them to springs of living water. And God will wipe away every tear from their eyes (Revelation 7:17 NIV).

Another hymn by Fanny Crosby is found on page 173.

Art Thou Sunk
in Depths of Sorrow?

Art thou sunk in depths of sorrow
Where no arm can reach so low?
There is one whose arms almighty
Reach beyond thy deepest woe.
God th' eternal is thy refuge,
Let it still thy wild alarms;
Underneath thy deepest sorrow
Are the everlasting arms.

Underneath thee, underneath thee
Are the everlasting arms.
Everlasting, everlasting
Are the everlasting arms.

Other arms grow faint and weary,
These can never faint, nor fail;
Others reach our mounts of blessing,
These our lowest loneliest vale.
O that all might know his friendship!

O that all might see his charms!
O that all might have beneath them
Jesus' everlasting arms.

Underneath us, O how easy;
We have not to mount on high,
But to sink into his fulness,
And in trustful weakness lie.
And we find our humbling failures
Save us from the strength that harms!
We may fail, but underneath us
Are the everlasting arms.

Arms of Jesus! fold me closer,
To thy strong and loving breast,
Till my spirit on thy bosom
Finds its everlasting rest;
And when time's last sands are sinking,
Shield my heart from all alarms,
Softly whispering, "Underneath thee
Are the everlasting arms."

A. B. SIMPSON (1843–1919)

31

There is none like unto the God of
Jeshurun, who rideth upon the heaven in
thy help, and in his excellency on the sky.
The eternal God is thy refuge, and under-
neath are the everlasting arms: and he
shall thrust out the enemy from before
thee; and shall say, Destroy them. Israel
then shall dwell in safety alone: the foun-
tain of Jacob shall be upon a land of corn
and wine; also his heavens shall drop
down dew (Deuteronomy 33:26–28 KJV).

The first complete Bible commentary in English was written by Matthew Henry, who said this about Deuteronomy 33:26: "When we are expecting that God should bless us by doing well for us, we must bless him by speaking well of him."

In ancient days everyone had a favorite god. Nations, cities, towns, communities, and families all boasted of their own god. But in the preceding verses Moses speaks well of God by declaring the preeminence of the God of

Jeshurun (Israel) above all such gods.

First, Moses shows that God is literally above all. God does not simply ride *through* heaven, God rides "upon the heaven in thy help, and in his excellency on the sky" (v. 26). "Riding upon heaven," God manages and directs the heavenly realm like a champion equestrian. Matthew Henry says, "When he has anything to do for his people he rides upon the heavens to do it; for he does it swiftly and strongly: no enemy can either anticipate or obstruct the progress of him that rides on the heavens."

Second, though other gods are homemade and easily discarded, ours is the eternal God with everlasting arms that uphold the believers (v. 27). These support the believers with protection, safety, and security. But they are not physical arms. They are the encircling arms of God's endless love; they are the strong arms of the everlasting covenant; they are the saving arms of eternal redemption. The arms of God's love uphold the entire world. The arms of the new covenant support his church. And the arms of

Christ's redemption extend under each and every believer to bear them up in their afflictions, temptations, and trials.

PRAYER

Arms of Jesus! fold me closer
To thy strong and loving breast,
Till my spirit on thy bosom
Finds its everlasting rest.

Lord, help me to find more compassion
in my heart for the world
around me because of your love.
Give me confidence in the fulfillment
of your purpose in the church
because of the unchangeable covenant.
Help me commit myself more fully to Christ
because of his death and resurrection.

Other hymns by A. B. Simpson are found on pages 40 and 141.

BE STILL, MY HEART

Be still, my heart! These anxious cares
To thee are burdens, thorns, and snares;
They cast dishonor on the Lord,
And contradict his gracious Word.

Brought safely by his hand thus far,
Why wilt thou now give place to fear?
How canst thou want if he provide,
Or lose thy way with such a guide?

When first before his mercy seat
Thou didst to him thine all commit;
He gave thee warrant from that hour
To trust his wisdom, love, and power.

Did ever trouble yet befall,
And he refuse to hear thy call?
And has he not his promise passed,
That thou shalt overcome at last?

He who has helped me hitherto
Will help me all my journey through,
And give me daily cause to raise
New Ebenezers to his praise.

Though rough and thorny be the road,
It leads thee on, apace, to God;
Then count thy present trials small,
For God will make amends for all.

JOHN NEWTON (1725–1807)

Scripture tells us not to be anxious (see Philippians 4:6) and to cast all our cares on the Lord in prayer and supplication with thanksgiving (see 1 Peter 5:7). Once we do that, the peace of God that exceeds all comprehension will guard our hearts and minds in Christ. John Newton, while scolding his unbelieving heart, says that neglecting this allows anxious cares to grow and ripen into burdens, thorns, and snares. These dishonor the Lord and repudiate God's gracious Word.

Remember when you first believed in Jesus

Christ and took him to be your Savior? You understood that he broke the power of death and opened the way to everlasting life through the gospel. At that moment God gave you the ability to trust the divine wisdom, love, and power. Weren't you absolutely sure that he was able to guard your life, your soul, until the day of his return (see 2 Timothy 1:1–12)? Mark that turning point, that crucial event, for it is your Ebenezer—your stone of help.

People in ancient days set up stone monuments when life-changing events occurred. On the night when Jacob lay down on a stone at Bethel he dreamed he saw a ladder extending to heaven. There he saw the Lord, and he was given the covenant that was previously promised to his father and grandfather. The next morning he got up very early, took the stone he had used as a bed, and set it up as a memorial pillar. Jacob called the place Bethel and made a vow to the Lord: "This stone that I have set up as a pillar will be God's house" (see Genesis 28:10–22 NIV).

Joshua did the same thing when the Promised Land finally belonged to Israel. He warned the people, "If you forsake the Lord and serve other gods, he will turn against you and destroy you, even though he has been so good to you."

But the people answered, "No, we are determined to serve the Lord!"

So Joshua made a covenant with the people of Israel and they committed themselves to the Lord. As a reminder of this agreement, he took a huge stone and rolled it beneath an oak tree beside the tabernacle. Joshua said to the people, "This stone has heard everything the Lord said to us. It will be a witness to testify against you if you go back on your word to God" (see Joshua 24:20–27).

These stones each marked a very important event in the history of Israel. A third stone was set up by Samuel when Israel recaptured the ark of the covenant from the Philistines. "Then Samuel took a stone and set it up between Mizpah and Shen, and called its name Ebenezer, saying, 'Thus far the Lord has helped us' " (1 Samuel 7:12 NKJV). *Ebenezer* means "stone of help."

MEDITATION

Look back on the landscape of your life and focus on the many stones of help that are standing there. These Ebenezers say, "God who has helped you up to this time will help you all through your journey." Let this certainty alone give you cause to raise a new Ebenezer to his praise.

Other hymns by John Newton are found on pages 45 and 195.

BE STILL, O TROUBLED SOUL

O troubled soul, beneath the rod
Thy Father speaks—be still, be still;
Learn to be silent unto God,
And let him mold thee to his will.

Be still, O troubled soul, be still;
Bear not, thy Father's arms enfold thee.
Take up thy cross, lay down thy will;
Be silent unto God, and let him mold thee.

O anxious soul, lay down thy load,
Oh, hear his voice, he speaks to thee,
"Be still and know that I am God,
And cast thy every care on me."

O fearful soul, be still, be still,
Be of good cheer; has he not said,
"I will be with you, fear no ill,
'Tis I, 'tis I, be not afraid"?

O praying soul, be still, be still,
He cannot break his plighted word;
Sink down into his blessed will,
And wait in patience on the Lord.

O waiting soul, be still, be strong,
And though he tarry, trust and wait;
Doubt not, he will not wait too long,
Fear not, he will not come too late.

A. B. SIMPSON (1843–1919)

I remember the first person I ever saw bow down on both knees to pray. He was a well-liked man whom I didn't find to be self-righteous, he held a good job, and he had a picture-book family—four children in the care of his bright and beautiful wife.

Yet his family life soon came to resemble many in modern America. His first child grew into adolescence and became unruly. She ceased to talk with him or his wife, stayed away from the house, and neglected her schoolwork. She brought a broad streak of chaos into this praying man's family and they all traveled a long, rough patch of road.

It goes without saying that my friend prayed for his daughter, but it seemed that with each prayer events worsened. He would absorb the impact of the disappointment, the fear for his child, the effect on the family, and pray again. And again, things would degenerate.

This downward spiral continued for two or three years until one day my praying friend stopped praying, exhausted. He knew well the promises of Luke 11, that everyone who asks, receives; everyone who seeks, finds; and that the door is opened to everyone who knocks (v. 10). These formerly were customary experiences for him, but he had said it all to God in prayer. He had nothing more to ask for. It was as if he had been knocking on an actual door and the skin of his knuckles had worn away. No more knocking for him.

He wasn't bitter or angry at God. He didn't leave the faith, fall from grace, or backslide into sin. He did not give up on his daughter. There simply was no more prayer in him. I think God had forced my friend to stop his many prayers, saying, "O praying soul, be still, be still."

This man, figuratively speaking, had asked for a fish. Was he given a snake instead? He asked for an egg. Had he found a scorpion (v. 12)? Just as he knew how to give good gifts to his children, so I witnessed the heavenly Father give him the Holy Spirit in answer to his prayers (v. 13).

The Holy Spirit helps us in our distress. When my friend didn't know what he should pray for, when he didn't know how to pray anymore, the Spirit prayed for him in ways that cannot be expressed in words (Romans 8:26). This pleading of the Spirit is fully in harmony with God's will (v. 27). This is how "God causes everything to work together for the good of those who love God and are called according to his purpose for them" (v. 28 NLT).

PRAYER

*Dearest Lord, may I also learn to sink
down into your blessed will and wait for
you in patience.*

Other hymns by A. B. Simpson are found on pages 30
and 141.

BEGONE, UNBELIEF, MY SAVIOR IS NEAR

Begone, unbelief, my Savior is near,
And for my relief will surely appear;
By prayer let me wrestle, and he will perform;
With Christ in the vessel, I smile at the storm.

Though dark be my way, since he is my guide,
'Tis mine to obey, 'tis his to provide;
Though cisterns be broken, and creatures
*   all fail,*
The word he hath spoke shall surely prevail.

His love, in time past, forbids me to think
He'll leave me at last in trouble to sink:
Each sweet Ebenezer I have in review
Confirms his good pleasure to help me
*   quite through.*

Why should I complain of want or distress,
Temptation or pain? He told me no less;

The heirs of salvation, I know from his Word,
Through much tribulation must follow
    their Lord.

How bitter that cup no heart can conceive,
Which he drank quite up, that sinners
    might live!
His way was much rougher and darker
    than mine;
Did Christ, my Lord, suffer, and shall
    I repine?

Since all that I meet shall work for my good,
The bitter is sweet, the medicine, food;
Though painful at present, 'twill cease
    before long,
And then, oh, how pleasant the conqueror's
    song.

JOHN NEWTON (1725–1807)

"Go west to the land of Cyprus; go east to
the land of Kedar. Think about what you
see there. See if anyone has ever heard of

anything as strange as this. Has any nation ever exchanged its gods for another god, even though its gods are nothing? Yet my people have exchanged their glorious God for worthless idols! The heavens are shocked at such a thing and shrink back in horror and dismay, says the LORD. For my people have done two evil things: They have forsaken me—the fountain of living water. And they have dug for themselves cracked cisterns that can hold no water at all!" (Jeremiah 2:10–13, NLT).

"Begone unbelief!" commands John Newton. "With Christ in the vessel, I smile at the storm." Newton is referring to the time when Jesus and the disciples were in a boat crossing the Sea of Galilee. Suddenly, a terrible storm blew up and waves began to break into the boat. The disciples were terrified but Jesus was peacefully sleeping. The disciples woke him up, shouting, "Lord, save us! We're going to drown!" Jesus responded, "Why are you afraid? You have so little faith!"

Then he stood and defied the wind and waves and suddenly the sea was calm. The disciples were in awe. "Who is this man?" they asked each other. "Even the wind and waves obey him!" (See Matthew 8:23–27.)

The disciples had Christ in their vessel— everybody was in the same boat. But when the storm came up, the disciples believed more in the storm than they did in the Lord. Consequently, Jesus rebuked them—"You have so little faith!" In this is found the meaning of unbelief—or believing in something other than Christ.

While this is a dramatic example, life presents more humdrum styles of unbelief. Pick one out of the following list or supply your own (remember, unbelief is actually faith—but faith in something other than Christ): faith in money; faith in health; faith in youth, strength, or beauty; faith in politics, government, national leaders; faith in family; faith in a church, pastor, teaching, or doctrine; faith in a storm, crisis, or failure; faith in a bad decision or in dire straits.

You get the idea? It is natural to believe that

these hold sway in this life.

Jeremiah drew a word picture to show how Israel did this very thing. "They have forsaken me—the fountain of living water. And they have dug for themselves cracked cisterns that can hold no water at all!" (Jeremiah 2:13 NLT). A cistern is a pool designed to catch rainwater for household use. These are still used in developing countries that have no water distribution system. A cistern is usually a small pool, cemented and lined with stones. It may have a cover to prevent evaporation in arid climates.

Think about Jeremiah's picture. The people could have drawn water from a fresh-flowing spring. Instead, they searched for stale water at the bottom of a leaky cistern. This vivid easy-to-remember image can help those of us who tend toward unbelief—that is, just about everyone.

In his hymn, Newton wrote, "With Christ in the vessel, I smile at the storm." I like this. He didn't disturb Christ like the disciples. He didn't beg the Lord to stand and command the waves to be calm. Rather, Newton believed in

the holy one who was sailing along with him
and smiled at the storm.

MEDITATION

You have turned my mourning into danc-
ing; you have taken off my sackcloth and
clothed me with joy, so that my soul may
praise you and not be silent. O LORD my
God, I will give thanks to you forever
(Psalm 30:11, 12 NRSV).

Other hymns by John Newton are found on pages 35 and
195.

Count Your Blessings

When upon life's billows you are tempest tossed,
When you are discouraged, thinking all is lost,
Count your many blessings, name them one
 by one,
And it will surprise you what the Lord
 hath done.

Count your blessings, name them one by one;
Count your blessings, see what God hath done!
Count your blessings, name them one by one,
And it will surprise you what the Lord
 hath done.

Are you ever burdened with a load of care?
Does the cross seem heavy you are called
 to bear?
Count your many blessings, every doubt
 will fly,
And you will keep singing as the days go by.

When you look at others with their lands
    and gold,
Think that Christ has promised you his
    wealth untold;
Count your many blessings. Wealth can
    never buy
Your reward in heaven, nor your home
    on high.

So, amid the conflict whether great or small,
Do not be disheartened, God is over all;
Count your many blessings, angels will
    attend,
Help and comfort give you to your
    journey's end.

JOHNSON OATMAN, JR. (1856–1922)

I am thankful I was born and raised in the wealthiest country in the world, and that I have had good opportunities, fine children, and a long marriage. Still, I sometimes identify with Jacob. He wandered about the land and muddled through life until the day he prayed to God: "I am not worthy of all the faithfulness and unfailing love you have shown to me, your servant. When I left home, I owned nothing except a walking stick, and now my household fills two camps" (Genesis 32:10 NLT). Although Jacob was thankful for all he had and truly treasured God's love, the household that filled two camps caused him trouble to his dying day.

What strengthened Jacob through his troubles? If he were to count his blessings honestly, what would they be? His numerous sons? His several wives? All his possessions? No, Jacob would count two items. First, the promise that God gave to Abraham, repeated to Jacob's father Isaac, and retold to Jacob himself (see Genesis 28:13–15). Second, he would likely remember his personal encounter with God at Peniel (see 32:22–32).

You and I have promises from God as well. Some of these promised blessings are listed in Ephesians 1:3–14. Read them. If you believe the promises of the gospel of Jesus Christ, you are blessed. If not, make this your prayer until God gives you understanding and faith in the gospel:

> *Father of my Lord Jesus Christ, give me spiritual wisdom and understanding so that I can grow in the knowledge of God. I pray that my heart will be flooded with light so that I can understand the wonderful future you have promised. I want to realize what a rich and glorious inheritance you have given to your people. I pray that I can begin to understand the incredible greatness of your power for those who believe you, the same mighty power that raised Christ from the dead (see Ephesians 1:17–20).*

Our personal encounter with Jesus Christ is number two on the list of blessings. After the apostle Paul met the Lord on the road to Damascus (see Acts 26:9–18), he was never disobedient to that heavenly vision (v. 19). It stuck with him his entire life. Like Paul and Jacob, you will know if you have ever met Christ. If you are not sure you have had such an encounter, pray this prayer:

> *I pray, O God, that from your glorious, unlimited resources you will give me inner strength through the Holy Spirit. And I pray that Christ will make his home in my heart as I trust in him. Cause my roots to go down deep into the soil of your marvelous love.*
>
> *Give me the power to understand how wide, how long, how high, and how deep your love is. Let me experience the love of Christ, though it is so great I will never fully understand it. I want your mighty power to work within me so you can accomplish infinitely more than I would ever dare to ask or hope (see Ephesians 3:16–20).*

Use this prayer every day until you have an experience as intense as Jacob at Peniel or Paul on his way to Damascus.

PRAYER

Father, let me see the blessings in my life that have eternal value—my faith in the promises of your glorious gospel and my personal experience of your Son Jesus Christ.

DAY BY DAY

Day by day, and with each passing moment,
Strength I find to meet my trials here;
Trusting in my Father's wise bestowment,
I've no cause for worry or for fear.
He whose heart is kind beyond all measure
Gives unto each day what he deems best—
Lovingly, its part of pain and pleasure,
Mingling toil with peace and rest.

Every day, the Lord himself is near me
With a special mercy for each hour;
All my cares he fain would bear, and cheer me,
He whose name is Counselor and Power;
The protection of his child and treasure
Is a charge that on himself he laid;
"As thy days, thy strength shall be in measure,"
This the pledge to me he made.

Help me then, in every tribulation
So to trust thy promises, O Lord,

That I lose not faith's sweet consolation
Offered me within thy holy Word.
Help me, Lord, when toil and trouble meeting,
Ever to take, as from a father's hand,
One by one, the days, the moments fleeting,
Till I reach the promised land.

KAROLINA WILHELMINA SANDELL-BERG

(1832–1903)

Karolina Sandell grew up in Fröderyd, Sweden, the daughter of a Lutheran pastor. She was twenty-six when she accompanied her father on an ill-fated boat trip to Gothenberg. When the boat tipped suddenly, the father fell overboard and drowned as his daughter looked on. This tragedy shocked Karolina profoundly, but she went on and, as time went by, wrote more than 650 lyrics and hymns. Many of these are steeped in the memory of the dreadful loss of her father.

"Day by Day" makes known the place where consolation is found: "Help me then, in every tribulation so to trust thy promises, O Lord.

PEACE LIKE A RIVER

That I lose not faith's sweet consolation offered me within thy holy Word."

Sandell did not learn this by herself. Rather, the apostle Paul carried this message to her just as he broadcast it to the whole world. He outdid us all in suffering with "far more imprisonments, with countless floggings, and often near death" (2 Corinthians 11:23 NRSV). Here are the details: "Five times I have received from the Jews the forty lashes minus one. Three times I was beaten with rods. Once I received a stoning. Three times I was shipwrecked; for a night and a day I was adrift at sea; on frequent journeys, in danger from rivers, danger from bandits, danger from my own people, danger from Gentiles, danger in the city, danger in the wilderness, danger at sea, danger from false brothers and sisters; in toil and hardship, through many a sleepless night, hungry and thirsty, often without food, cold and naked. And, besides other things, I am under daily pressure because of my anxiety for all the churches" (vv. 24–28 NRSV).

Paul sums all this up in one sentence "We

were so utterly, unbearably crushed that we despaired of life itself" (2 Corinthians 1:8 NRSV). The extreme nature of the apostle's circumstances drove him to find the absolute, ultimate encouragement: "Indeed we felt that we had received the sentence of death. . ." And now comes the consolation, the encouragement, the motivation of our faith in Christ: ". . .so that we would rely not on ourselves but on God who raises the dead" (v. 9 NRSV).

Until the Lord's Second Coming, it is certain that everyone will die. But the consoling promise of the holy Word is that "in a moment, in the twinkling of an eye, at the last trumpet. . . the dead will be raised imperishable. . .then the saying that is written will be fulfilled: 'Death has been swallowed up in victory'" (1 Corinthians 15:52, 54 NRSV).

PRAYER

Jesus, I believe in you. You are the Resurrection and the Life. And even though I will die, I trust you that I will live again.

Deep Down into the Depths of this Thy Name

Deep down into the depths of this thy name,
My God, I sink and dwell in calm delight;
Thou art enough however long the day,
Thou art enough however dark the night.

Thou art my God—the All-Sufficient One,
Thou canst create for me whate'er I lack;
Thy mighty hand has strewn the lonely track
With miracles of love and tender care

For me thy trusting one. My God, I dare
Once more to fling myself upon thy breast,
And there adore thy ways in faith's deep rest,
And there adore thy ways in faith's quiet rest.

M. E. Barber (1866–1930)

The author of this hymn was born the daughter of a wheelwright in Peasenhall, County Suffolk, England. Later she would serve as a missionary near Foochow, China. Once a visitor to Barber's home asked her, "What are the requirements to work for the Lord?" She replied, "The requirement to work for the Lord is not to work."

Throughout her tenure in China, Barber lived in a small village and showed no ambition to seek fame in a larger venue such as Foochow. No doubt this is why Margaret Barber is so little known today. Her protégé, the evangelist and teacher Watchman Nee, remembered his teacher praying, "Lord, I am willing to break my heart in order that I may satisfy thy heart!"

Some of Barber's many poems have been set to music as hymns. Here is a verse that expresses the sentiment of Nee's remembrance:

If the path I travel lead me to the cross,
If the way thou choosest lead to pain and loss,
Let the compensation daily, hourly be
Shadowless communion, blessed Lord, with thee.

The hymn "Deep Down into the Depths of this Thy Name" tells the secret of how to travel such a path: Sink deep down into the depths of the Lord's name. But how do we do this? Speak the name. Would you do this now? Breathe the name—*Jesus*. Again—*Jesus*. When you need comfort on your life's path, say the name—*Jesus*.

After the victory of the cross and the triumph of the resurrection, God placed the name *Jesus* above every other name (see Philippians 2:6–11). This is why everyone who calls on the name of the Lord will be saved (see Romans 10:10). The Book of Acts has this to say about the name: "I will cause wonders in the heavens above and signs on the earth below—blood and fire and clouds of smoke. The sun will be turned into darkness, and the moon will turn bloodred, before that great and glorious day of the Lord arrives. And anyone who calls on the name of the Lord will be saved" (Acts 2:19–21 NLT).

MEDITATION

*Since the Lord's name is potent enough to
save people from the tribulations of the
last days, surely it can comfort you today.
God's salvation is not only eternal, but it
is also day to day.*

Another hymn by M. E. Barber is found on page 184.

DOES JESUS CARE?

Does Jesus care when my heart is pained
Too deeply for mirth or song,
As the burdens press, and the cares distress
And the way grows weary and long?

Oh yes, he cares, I know he cares,
His heart is touched with my grief;
When the days are weary, the long
    nights dreary,
I know my Savior cares.

Does Jesus care when my way is dark
With a nameless dread and fear?
As the daylight fades into deep night shades,
Does he care enough to be near?

Does Jesus care when I've tried and failed
To resist some temptation strong;
When for my deep grief there is no relief,
Though my tears flow all the night long?

Does Jesus care when I've said "good-bye"
To the dearest on earth to me,
And my sad heart aches till it nearly breaks,
Is it aught to him? Does he see?

FRANK E. GRAEFF (1860–1919)

When I thought about what I might write about this hymn, I had to pause. Soon I found myself wandering about my house, running my hand through my hair, murmuring, "Does Jesus care? Does Jesus care?" So I put on my cap and jacket and left the house to take a walk on a sunny winter's day.

I've been married a long time, and my wife and I have raised four children. As the old blues song says, "I've seen good times. I've seen bad times. I've had my share of hard times." Through it all I know that God has cared for me. But when I sat down to write about this hymn I couldn't simply knock off a cheery little article about God's care.

The reason is that I've tasted something of each verse in this hymn. Perhaps you have, as well. My heart has felt pain, my way has been dark, I've tried and failed, and I've said "good-bye forever" to people I love. But please don't think I'm boasting. This does not make me special or spiritual. Because as often as pain and fear and loss have touched me, I've asked, "Does God see what's happening here? Is this meaningful to the one in whom I've placed my faith?"

If you have never had such thoughts, I say to you, just wait.

Frank Graeff, the author of this hymn, was a Methodist pastor in Philadelphia, Pennsylvania. Known as the "Sunshine Minister," Graeff had a simple faith that made him a special friend of children and an encouragement to everyone who knew him. Still, he doubted. Once when he was despondent and in physical pain he went to the Bible and read, "Casting all your care upon him, for he careth for you" (1 Peter 5:7 KJV). After meditating on these words, Graeff wrote this hymn.

The Bible gives clear instructions about what

people should do with their troubles: "Cast your cares on him." Throw them over onto Christ. After all, he is the man of suffering who is acquainted with grief (see Isaiah 53:3). Suffering is nothing new to him. In this world troubles never cease. Yet Christ assures you, "Take courage; I have conquered the world" (John 16:33 NRSV). His death and resurrection have equipped him with an infinite capacity for caring.

PRAYER

Dearest Lord Jesus, at this moment I cast my cares on you. I give you this one: _____; and this one: _____; and this one, too: _____. Care for me, Jesus, care for me today.

GOD HOLDS THE KEY
OF ALL UNKNOWN

God holds the key of all unknown,
And I am glad;
If other hands should hold the key,
Or if he trusted it to me,
I might be sad.

What if tomorrow's cares were here,
Without its rest?
I'd rather he unlocked the day,
And, as the hours swing open, say,
My will is best.

The very dimness of my sight
Makes me secure;
For, groping in my misty way,
I feel his hand; I hear him say,
My help is sure.

I cannot read his future plans;

But this I know:
I have the smiling of his face,
And all the refuge of his grace
While here below.

Enough; this covers all my wants;
And so I rest;
For what I cannot, he can see,
And in his care I, saved, shall be
Forever blest.

J. Parker

Despite all plans, the future is unknown. We plan for today, we plan for tomorrow, and some of us even have the luxury of setting aside funds for retirement. About our habit of planning ahead James says, "Look here, you people who say, 'Today or tomorrow we are going to a certain town and will stay there a year. We will do business there and make a profit.' How do you know what will happen tomorrow? For your life is like the morning fog—it's here a little while, then it's gone. What you ought to say is, 'If the

Lord wants us to, we will live and do this or that.' Otherwise you will be boasting about your own plans, and all such boasting is evil" (James 4:13–16 NLT).

It seems to me that James is not telling us to stop making plans. Rather, he tells us to be humble before God and acknowledge God's control of all, including our little lives.

The man called Job had a pretty good retirement plan—he had seven sons and three daughters, owned 7,000 sheep, 3,000 camels, 500 teams of oxen, and 500 female donkeys, and employed many servants. The richest person in the region (see Job 1:2, 3), Job lost everything he possessed in a day.

God considered Job the finest man in all the earth—a man of complete integrity who feared God and had nothing to do with evil (Job 1:8). But God's plans for Job were entirely different from Job's plans for himself. When his wife advised him to curse God and die, Job, who truly loved God, told her, "Shall we receive the good at the hand of God, and not receive the bad?" (2:10 NRSV). The story of Job is so extreme so that not one of us can say we have suffered more than he. As the Book of Job proceeds, Job comes to his senses and more clearly sees his place in God's plan.

I once knew a pastor who did not really know the Lord. A good and hard-working man, he felt that God had called him to his vocation. Yet there was something missing and he didn't know it and neither did anyone else. But God knew—and then suffering came. This man's father, whom he loved dearly, was diagnosed with leukemia and quickly died. In grief the pastor turned to the Lord and unexpectedly found himself born again! Though he was surprised and joyous at the filling of the Holy Spirit, he was also dispirited to learn that for so many years he had not personally known the Lord. It was as if, in his ministry, he had said, "Today or tomorrow we are going to a certain town and will stay there a year" without truly acknowledging that God holds the future.

When suffering opened the door for this

pastor to know the Lord, he could join Job in saying these wonderful words: "I have uttered what I did not understand, things too wonderful for me, which I did not know. . . . I had heard of you by the hearing of the ear, but now my eye sees you" (Job 42:3, 5 NRSV).

PRAYER

Lord, forgive me that I, too, often utter what I do not understand. I pray you, please replace my hearing about you and my learning about you with a true vision of you. Give me the revelation of Jesus Christ.

God Moves in a Mysterious Way

God moves in a mysterious way
His wonders to perform;
He plants his footsteps in the sea
And rides upon the storm.

Deep in unfathomable mines
Of never failing skill,
He treasures up his bright designs
And works his sovereign will.

Ye fearful saints, fresh courage take;
The clouds ye so much dread
Are big with mercy and shall break
In blessings on your head.

Judge not the Lord by feeble sense,
But trust him for his grace;
Behind a frowning providence
He hides a smiling face.

His purposes will ripen fast,
Unfolding every hour;
The bud may have a bitter taste,
But sweet will be the flower.

Blind unbelief is sure to err
And scan his work in vain;
God is his own interpreter,
And he will make it plain.

WILLIAM COWPER (1731–1800)

Poet William Cowper was related to the great seventeenth-century poet and preacher John Donne and his father was chaplain to King George II. Cowper (pronounced "Cooper") himself, though, was seriously depressed and spent years searching for recovery. "I was a stricken deer that had left the herd," he explained. While Cowper was hospitalized for his mental condition, he took to reading the Bible and found faith in Christ.

Based on the following story, "God Moves in a Mysterious Way" is (erroneously, I believe) assumed by many to be the last hymn Cowper wrote.

> *William Cowper struggled with chronic depression and one night, deceived by his depression, he decided to commit suicide by drowning. So he called a cab and told the driver to take him to the Thames River. However, thick fog came in and prevented the driver from finding the river. After driving around for a while, the cab driver gave up and Cowper stepped out of the cab. To his great surprise, he found himself back on his own doorstep. God, in a mysterious way, had sent the fog to prevent him from killing himself.*

This story fails on two counts. First, Cowper didn't live in London when he wrote his hymns. He lived in Olney, Buckinghamshire, where he collaborated in writing hymns with John Newton, the author of "Amazing Grace." Second, there is no way that the driver of a

London hack would not be able to find the Thames River even in the thickest fog.

Still, it is true that God works in mysterious ways. There was once a man who received great visions and revelations from the Lord. This man was caught up into the third heaven either in body or spirit, he wasn't sure. But he did know that he was caught up into paradise and heard things so astounding that they cannot be repeated. This man was the apostle Paul (see 2 Corinthians 12:1–4).

Like William Cowper, Paul had his own peculiar weaknesses. Even though he had received wonderful revelations from God, he was given a "thorn in his flesh" or a disability of sorts to torment him and keep him from becoming proud. And though Paul continually begged the Lord to take the thorn away, God refused, saying, "My grace is all you need. My power works best in your weakness."

Now here is a mystery: Why is there no easy, miraculous way out of our troubles? Why, instead of the convenient way of suicide, did

Cowper find himself back on his own doorstep, back in his own life and troubles? Even the great apostle was trapped in his circumstances. Paul explains: "I am glad to boast about my weaknesses, so that the power of Christ may work through me. Since I know it is all for Christ's good, I am quite content with my weaknesses and with insults, hardships, persecutions, and calamities. For when I am weak, then I am strong" (2 Corinthians 12:9–10 NLT).

PRAYER

Lord, let me see and acknowledge my weaknesses. And then, as the Scripture says, may I be content with them—may I accept them. And Lord, at the same time, please give the grace to know that when I am weak, then I am strong.

Another hymn by William Cowper is found on page 178.

GOD WILL TAKE CARE OF YOU

Be not dismayed whatever betide,
God will take care of you;
Beneath his wings of love abide,
God will take care of you.

God will take care of you,
Through every day, o'er all the way;
He will take care of you,
God will take care of you.

Through days of toil when heart doth fail,
God will take care of you;
When dangers fierce your path assail,
God will take care of you.

All you may need he will provide,
God will take care of you;
Nothing you ask will be denied,
God will take care of you.

No matter what may be the test,
God will take care of you;
Lean, weary one, upon His breast,
God will take care of you.

CIVILLA DURFEE MARTIN (1866–1948)

The Old Testament Book of Ruth is a wonderful illustration of this hymn. Ruth, the eighth book of the Bible, is found right after Judges. Read it slowly; read it out loud; read it to someone you love. You will soon discover how to abide beneath the wings of God's love.

Death claimed the three men most important to Ruth—her father-in-law, husband, and brother-in-law. Consequently, three women were left destitute—Ruth, her sister-in-law Orpah, and her mother-in-law Naomi. As Naomi departs to find refuge with her relatives in Israel, she advises Orpah and Ruth to stay behind in their homeland of Moab. Orpah agrees to turn back while Ruth clings to Naomi saying, "I will go wherever you go and live wherever you live. Your people will be my people, and your God will be my God" (Ruth 1:16 NLT).

Ruth was in a desperate situation. In those days women could own no property and were entirely dependent upon their husbands. Moreover, Ruth's culture treated widows as castaways, never to be married again. Ruth's words to Naomi show that she knew things looked bad: "I will die where you die and will be buried there" (v. 17 NLT).

But it was worse than Ruth knew. Because her people, the Moabites, had resisted Israel as they journeyed through the wilderness, God commanded the following: "No Ammonites or Moabites, or any of their descendants for ten generations, may be included in the assembly of the Lord. . . . You must never, as long as you live, try to help [them] in any way" (Deuteronomy 23:3, 6 NLT). So, you see, Ruth's situation was about as bad as can be. This is why her story sheds light on every case of suffering and need, proving the hymnist's words, "God will take care of you."

"So Naomi returned from Moab, accompanied by her daughter-in-law Ruth," this young, hopeless Moabite woman. They arrived in Bethlehem at the beginning of the barley harvest (see Ruth 1:22) and Ruth immediately went to work gleaning the harvest. To *glean* means to gather up the leftovers—that which the reapers leave at the edges of the field or drop as they go along. Gleanings are the leftovers for the very poor. If this were a modern story, Ruth might be digging through a Dumpster behind a supermarket.

Consider Ruth, the daughter of a cursed tribe, a young widow with no prospects, reduced to culling what others did not need. Yet she had one thing going for her: She had attached herself to Naomi, a child of Israel and believer in the one God. As a result, Ruth found her redeemer.

It so happened that Ruth was working in fields that belonged to her dead husband's relative, a man named Boaz. And it seems that almost immediately Boaz loved her and began to take care of her. He said to her, "May the Lord, the God of Israel, under whose wings you

have come to take refuge, reward you fully"
(Ruth 2:12 NLT).

Ruth's story resonates in my heart as I was
once nearly as desperate as she. And although I
felt I had no right to do so, I began to pray a little each day. These prayers were as pathetic as
Ruth's gleanings, yet the Redeemer took notice
of me and loved me. Then one night I asked
Jesus Christ, "Spread your cloak over me, for you
are my redeemer" (see Ruth 3:9). At that
moment the Sun of Righteousness arose in me
with healing in his wings. And I went free, leap-
ing with joy like a calf let out to pasture (see
Malachi 4:2).

PRAYER

*Dear Lord Jesus Christ, thank you for
taking notice of me, and for spreading
your cloak of love over me. It is my joy to
remain here forever.*

HE FAILETH NOT

He faileth not, for he is God;
He faileth not, his grace how good;
He faileth not, his Word is clear;
If we have God, whom need we fear?

The highest mount, he can make plain;
The wildest flood, he can restrain!
God of impossibilities!
Poor puny man, now learn his ways.

The axe did swim on Jordan's wave!
Our God the Red Sea's waters clave!
He stopped the sun! made long the day!
This is the God to whom we pray.

He bars the sea with feeble sand!
The proud waves bow at his command!
If God is thine, what more your need?
Can he not work for you indeed?

Our God is love; your needs are known;
His promises he'll fully own.
Our gracious God bows down his ear
The feeblest, weakest cry to hear.

Our God is light, and never yet,
One promise did he e'er forget.
His promises in Christ the Son
Are fully pledged, yea and amen.

Our faithful God, faith cannot break,
Nor death, nor hell, his promise shake!
Who ask in faith, he'll not deny;
His word is sure, he must reply.

He faileth not, let all men hear;
He faileth not, his word is clear.
He faileth not, his grace how good;
He faileth not, for he is God!

ANONYMOUS

Long ago, in the days that are recorded in the Old Testament, God spoke many times and in many ways through the prophets. These included the writers of the histories of Israel, the poets of Scripture, and the writers we now call the major and minor prophets. Their speaking was absolutely true and wonderful. But now in the days of the New Testament, God has spoken to us through the Son. The only way people can truly know God is through the Son, Jesus Christ.

God promised everything to the Son, and through the Son the universe and everything in it was made. Jesus Christ reflects God's own glory; everything about Christ represents God exactly. After he died to cleanse us from sin, Christ sat down in honor at the right side of God. From this place of authority he sustains the entire universe. Now that's faithfulness! (See Hebrews 1:1–3.)

Since Christ sustains the universe, you can be sure that he never wavers between yes and no. Christ is the divine *Yes*—God's affirmation—because all of God's promises have been fulfilled in him. And in case you've ever wondered, this is why we say "Amen" during worship when we give glory to God through Christ (see 2 Corinthians 1:19, 20).

One sentence from this hymn expresses this perfectly—"His promises in Christ the Son are fully pledged, yea and amen." This is truth firmly founded in the New Testament. It is no longer necessary to look anywhere else for assurance of God's faithfulness.

Once Jesus went to a place called Caesarea Philippi, twenty or thirty miles north of the Sea of Galilee. Out of the hills of this remote district spring the headwaters of the Jordan River. When Jesus took his disciples there on a retreat, he asked this question: "Who do people say that the Son of Man is?"

They had various answers: "Some say John the Baptist, some say Elijah, and others say Jeremiah or one of the other prophets." These are good, positive answers, though they are incorrect. People saw Christ in other ways as well—he was a drunkard, a rebel, a heretic, and a criminal. To some he was a healer, a feeder of the hungry, a miracle worker, and more. But not one of these was the answer Jesus wanted.

Then he asked them, "Who do you say I am?"

Peter was the first to speak. "You are the Messiah, the Son of the living God," he said.

Hurrah! Somebody finally got it right.

"Peter," Jesus said, "you are blessed. You did not learn this from anyone other than my Father in heaven. God has revealed it to you" (see Matthew 16:13–17).

PRAYER

Lord Jesus, these days you are many different things to many people. But no matter what they think you are, give them the blessing of seeing that you are the Christ, the Son of the living God.

HE GIVETH MORE GRACE

He giveth more grace when the burdens
        grow greater,
He sendeth more strength when the labors
        increase,
To added affliction he addeth his mercy,
To multiplied trials, his multiplied peace.

When we have exhausted our store of
        endurance,
When our strength has failed ere the day
        is half-done,
When we reach the end of our hoarded resources,
Our Father's full giving is only begun.

His love has no limit, his grace has no measure,
His power no boundary known unto men,
For out of his infinite riches in Jesus,
He giveth and giveth and giveth again.

ANNIE JOHNSON FLINT (1866–1932)

The apostle Paul begins every one of his letters to the churches by saying, "Grace to you and peace from God our Father and the Lord Jesus Christ" (see Romans 1:7). The only variation is found in Paul's letters to Timothy which begin, "Grace, mercy, and peace. . ." (1 Timothy 1:2 NIV). There is no question about it: God's grace, mercy, and peace are ours, given freely as needed. Annie Flint's hymn assures us that when it comes to God, love has no limit, grace has no measure, and power no knowable boundary.

Think of a gift that expresses God's divine grace, mercy, and peace—such as "In the beginning God created the heavens and the earth" (Genesis 1:1). Every physical thing is derived from this first big gift, an act of unconstrained mercy.

Then there is the unfathomable gift of the Son, Jesus Christ, who is the chief topic of the Bible. Jesus is a gift to ponder and praise for a lifetime. "For God so loved the world, that he gave his only begotten Son, that whosoever believeth in him should not perish, but have everlasting life. For God sent not his Son into the world to condemn the world; but that the world through him might be saved" (John 3:16, 17 KJV).

Furthermore, God gives the Holy Spirit without limitation (John 3:34). Simply consider what Jesus said shortly before he went away to be crucified—"I have much more to say to you, more than you can now bear. But when he, the Spirit of truth, comes, he will guide you into all truth. He will not speak on his own; he will speak only what he hears, and he will tell you what is yet to come. He will bring glory to me by taking from what is mine and making it known to you" (John 16:12–14 NIV). Thank God for the Holy Spirit who makes Christ fully known!

Another of God's gifts is the church. It is full of the people who care for us both practically and spiritually. Romans chapter 16 gives a glimpse of this normal vitality among of the people of God's church. Such a church is the linchpin of God's eternal purpose. It is the product of the gospel that delivers the unsearchable riches of Christ. This is a mystery that was hidden in God from the beginning of the ages until now. Why is there such a gospel? So that the church can reveal to the rulers and authorities in the heavenly realms the complete wisdom of God. This, Paul tells us, is the eternal purpose that God accomplished in Christ Jesus our Lord (see Ephesians 3:8–11).

When all we now see has passed away, God will give us a final gift, an eternal dwelling place, the New Jerusalem. As it is written, "I John saw the holy city, new Jerusalem, coming down from God out of heaven, prepared as a bride adorned for her husband. And I heard a great voice out of heaven saying, Behold, the tabernacle of God is with men, and he will dwell with them, and they shall be his people, and God himself shall be with them, and be their God. And God shall wipe away all tears from their eyes; and there shall be no more death, neither sorrow, nor crying, neither shall there be any more pain: for the former things are passed away. And he that sat upon the throne said, Behold, I make all things new" (Revelation 21:2–5 KJV).

Thank you, dear God, that your love has no limit, your grace has no measure, your power has no known boundary. I open to all that you give and give and give again out of your infinite riches in Christ.

Another hymn by Annie Flint is found on page 216.

I KNOW NOT WHAT AWAITS ME

I know not what awaits me,
God kindly veils my eyes,
And o'er each step of my onward way
He makes new scenes to rise;
And every joy he sends me
Comes a sweet and glad surprise.

Where he may lead I'll follow,
My trust in him repose
And every hour in perfect peace,
I'll sing, "He knows, he knows."
And every hour in perfect peace,
I'll sing, "He knows, he knows."

One step I see before me,
'Tis all I need to see,
The light of heaven more brightly shines
When earth's illusions flee.
And sweetly through the silence comes,

His loving, "Trust in me!"

Oh, blissful lack of wisdom,
'Tis blessed not to know;
He holds me with his own right hand,
And will not let me go,
And lulls my troubled soul to rest
In him who loves me so.

So on I go not knowing;
I would not if I might;
I'd rather walk in the dark with God
Than go alone in the light;
I'd rather walk by faith with him
Than go alone by sight.

PHILIP PAUL BLISS (1838–1876)

At 7:28 P.M. on December 29, 1876, Train No. 5, the Pacific Express, made up of two locomotives, four express baggage cars, a smoking car, two coaches, a parlor car, and three sleeping cars, was bound westward in Ohio over the Lake Shore & Michigan Southern Railway. It was two hours behind schedule since a snow-storm had raged all the previous day and masses of snow drifted across the tracks. The wind was blowing at about forty miles per hour. On board were 156 souls, among them the hymnist Philip Paul Bliss, author of "Hallelujah! What a Savior," and his wife Lucy. But when the train reached the iron bridge that spanned the Ashtabula River, a quarter-mile east of the Ashtabula, Ohio, station, the bridge collapsed, sending the train plunging seventy feet into the chasm. Fires immediately broke out and swept through the wreckage. Ninety-two people per-ished, twenty-five of these burned beyond recognition, and sixty-four were injured. A few days later, Charles Collins, chief engineer of the bridge, committed suicide.

Lucy and Philip Bliss were returning that day from a Christmas visit to family in Rome, Pennsylvania. Their two young sons had stayed behind in Rome. Mr. Bliss initially escaped from the wreckage but was killed when he went back into the train to rescue his wife from the flames. Neither his body nor that of his wife was identified. When Bliss's trunk was salvaged from the wreckage, in it was found an unpublished hymn that began, "I know not what awaits me, God kindly veils my eyes. . . ."

At the time of his death, Philip Bliss was thirty-eight years old and had already written scores of hymns and sacred songs. Comparable to Ira Sankey and Fanny Crosby in his contribution to the church's hymnody, he wrote "Almost Persuaded," "Free From the Law, O Happy Condition," "I'm So Glad That Jesus Loves Me," and "There Is a Light in the Valley." Bliss must have had special insight into spiritual things. But the final words from his pen, "I know not what awaits me, God kindly veils my eyes. . . ," show that he was like us all. No one knows how or when they will die and the only thing that can interfere with anyone's death is Christ's return.

The apostle Paul was referring to this when he wrote, "But let me tell you a wonderful secret God has revealed to us. Not all of us will die, but we will all be transformed. It will happen in a moment, in the blinking of an eye, when the last trumpet is blown. For when the trumpet sounds, the Christians who have died will be raised with transformed bodies. And then we who are living will be transformed so that we will never die. For our perishable earthly bodies must be transformed into heavenly bodies that will never die. When this happens—when our perishable earthly bodies have been transformed into heavenly bodies that will never die—then at last the Scriptures will come true: 'Death is swallowed up in victory' " (1 Corinthians 15:51–54 NLT).

The unidentified remains retrieved at the site of the Ashtabula train disaster were placed in a common grave in the Ashtabula Cemetery. A memorial to Lucy and Philip Bliss was erected in the cemetery at Rome, Pennsylvania, on July 17, 1877.

PRAYER

*Lord Jesus Christ, I proceed not knowing
what awaits me in this life. And I do this
with thanksgiving, because I'd rather
walk in the dark with you than go all
alone in the light.*

I'm a Child of the King

My Father is rich in houses and lands,
He holdeth the wealth of the world in his hands!
Of rubies and diamonds, of silver and gold,
His coffers are full, he has riches untold.

I'm a child of the King,
A child of the King:
With Jesus my Savior,
I'm a child of the King.

My Father's own Son, the Savior of men,
Once wandered on earth as the poorest of them;
But now he is pleading our pardon on high,
That we may be his when he comes by and by.

I once was an outcast stranger on earth,
A sinner by choice, an alien by birth,
But I've been adopted, my name's written down,
An heir to a mansion, a robe and a crown.

A tent or a cottage, why should I care?
They're building a palace for me over there;
Though exiled from home, yet still may I sing:
All glory to God, I'm a child of the King.

HARRIET BUELL (1834–1910)

"And if children, then. . .heirs of God"
(Romans 8:17 KJV).

This hymn does its best to describe God's riches by using everyday symbols of wealth. Indeed, according to the words of the hymn, God is rich in houses and lands, and possesses the wealth of the world—rubies and diamonds, silver and gold. Thus, as "children of the King," believers in God are heirs to mansions, robes, crowns, and such.

Now I don't mean to detract from the faith of Harriet Buell or her love for God, but such a description of God is wholly inadequate. Look at the Book of Romans, for example, which provides a seamless, thorough description of the legitimacy and efficacy of God's work in Christ.

When Paul completed the portion of this book, which is in effect the legal document describing the love and justice of God's gospel (chapters 1–11), he cannot withhold his praise. "O the depth of the riches and wisdom and knowledge of God! How unsearchable are his judgments and how inscrutable his ways! 'For who has known the mind of the Lord? Or who has been his counselor?' 'Or who has given a gift to him, to receive a gift in return?' For from him and through him and to him are all things. To him be the glory forever. Amen" (Romans 11:33–36 NRSV).

There is no way to know the riches of God. They are beyond finding out—yet Paul took on the task. As he said, "Unto me, who am less than the least of all saints, is this grace given, that I should preach among the Gentiles the unsearchable riches of Christ" (Ephesians 3:8 KJV). And he did this, giving his life so that you and I and everyone else could see "what is the fellowship of the mystery, which from the beginning of the world hath been hid in God, who created all things by Jesus Christ" (v. 9 KJV). This is why the language of the New Testament, its unique words and phrases, is the only human language adequate to describe God and the person and work of Christ.

Let us sing the old hymns like Harriet Buell's. They encourage and delight the heart. But even more, let's be saturated with the words of Scripture that have been given to us with "the intent that now unto the principalities and powers in heavenly places might be known by the church the manifold wisdom of God" (v. 10 KJV).

MEDITATION

And I saw the holy city, the new Jerusalem, coming down from God out of heaven like a beautiful bride prepared for her husband. . . . The wall was made of jasper, and the city was pure gold, as clear as glass. The wall of the city was built on foundation stones inlaid with twelve gems: the first was jasper, the second sapphire, the third agate, the fourth emerald, the fifth onyx, the sixth carnelian, the

*seventh chrysolite, the eighth beryl, the
ninth topaz, the tenth chrysoprase, the
eleventh jacinth, the twelfth amethyst.
The twelve gates were made of pearls—
each gate from a single pearl! And the
main street was pure gold, as clear as
glass (Revelation 21:2, 18–21 NLT).*

IN THE HEART OF JESUS

In the heart of Jesus there is love for you,
Love most pure and tender, love most deep
        and true;
Why should you be lonely, why for friendship
        sigh,
When the heart of Jesus has a full supply?

In the mind of Jesus there is thought for you,
Warm as summer sunshine, sweet as morn-
        ing dew;
Why should you be fearful, why take anxious
        thought,
Since the mind of Jesus cares for those he bought?

In the field of Jesus there is work for you;
Such as even angels might rejoice to do;
Why stand idly sighing for some life-work
        grand,
While the field of Jesus seeks your reaping
        hand?

In the church of Jesus there's a place for you;
Glorious, bright, and joyous, right and
    peaceful, too;
Why then, like a wand'rer roam with
    weary pace,
If the church of Jesus holds for you a place?

A. PUGH

Lovers of God are known by God. This intimate knowledge is possible because Jesus Christ now lives, following his resurrection. A clear description of the resurrected Christ is given in the Book of Revelation: "When I turned to see who was speaking to me, I saw seven gold lampstands. And standing in the middle of the lampstands was the Son of Man. He was wearing a long robe with a gold sash across his chest. His head and his hair were white like wool, as white as snow. And his eyes were bright like flames of fire. His feet were as bright as bronze refined in a furnace, and his voice thundered like mighty ocean waves. He held seven stars in his right hand, and a sharp two-edged sword came from his mouth. And his face was as bright as the sun in all its brilliance" (Revelation 1:12–16 NLT).

How different this Son of Man is compared with the familiar Jesus Christ of the four Gospels! His death, burial, resurrection, and ascension to God's throne transfigured Jesus. At first glance he is terrifying. No wonder John fell down like he was dead (v. 17). Christ's eyes are flaming, his voice thunders like the sea, and his face is as bright as the sun. Still, Christ cares no less for us than he did in his time on earth. In fact, he is more fully empowered to care for his believers. This is why he is seen among the seven golden lampstands, which represent all the churches throughout history (v. 20).

Chapters two and three of Revelation show Jesus Christ caring for the churches. Since the church is simply believers gathered together, he is concerned for each believer in such a gathering. Here are seven verses that tell what Christ knows about us:

"*I know* your deeds, your hard work and

your perseverance. *I know* that you cannot tolerate wicked men, that you have tested those who claim to be apostles but are not, and have found them false" (Revelation 2:2 NIV). "*I know* your afflictions and your poverty—yet you are rich! *I know* the slander of those who say they are Jews and are not, but are a synagogue of Satan" (v. 9 NIV). "*I know* where you live—where Satan has his throne. Yet you remain true to my name. You did not renounce your faith in me, even in the days of Antipas, my faithful witness, who was put to death in your city—where Satan lives" (v. 13 NIV).

"*I know* your deeds, your love and faith, your service and perseverance, and that you are now doing more than you did at first" (v. 19 NIV). "*I know* your deeds; you have a reputation of being alive, but you are dead" (3:1 NIV). "*I know* your deeds. See, I have placed before you an open door that no one can shut. *I know* that you have little strength, yet you have kept my word and have not denied my name" (v. 8 NIV). "*I know* your deeds, that you are neither cold nor hot. I wish you were either one or the other!" (v.15 NIV).

What shall we do since Christ knows everything about us? I think that we must do as John did: "I am John, your brother" he affirmed. "In Jesus we are partners in suffering and in the Kingdom and in patient endurance" (Revelation 1:9 NLT). John was "in the Spirit" on the Lord's day (v. 10)—maybe he was praying, or singing, or meditating on Scripture—when he heard a loud voice behind him. Then he turned to see the one who was speaking to him. This is what we should do—turn to see the one who is speaking.

You may have heard the Lord speaking to you in one of the preceding seven verses. It may have been only one word, and it may have been frightening. Nonetheless, do as John did and turn in prayer to see the one who has spoken to you. This is how to experience the love of the resurrected Christ.

MEDITATION

"Anyone who is willing to hear should listen to the Spirit and understand what the Spirit is saying to the churches" (Revelation 3:22 NLT).

IN THE HOUR OF TRIAL

In the hour of trial, Jesus, plead for me,
Lest by base denial I depart from thee.
When thou seest me waver, with a look recall,
Nor for fear or favor suffer me to fall.

With forbidden pleasures would this vain
    world charm,
Or its sordid treasures spread to work me harm,
Bring to my remembrance sad Gethsemane,
Or, in darker semblance, cross-crowned
    Calvary.

Should thy mercy send me sorrow, toil and woe,
Or should pain attend me on my path below,
Grant that I may never fail thy hand to see;
Grant that I may ever cast my care on thee.

When my last hour cometh, fraught with
    strife and pain,
When my dust returneth to the dust again,

*On thy truth relying, through that
   mortal strife,
Jesus, take me, dying, to eternal life.*

JAMES MONTGOMERY (1771–1854)

Let's talk about the New Testament's original hour of trial. It began on the Mount of Olives shortly before Jesus was arrested. There he predicted that the disciples would renounce him. And as if his own words weren't enough, Jesus guaranteed they were true by quoting the prophecy of Zechariah 13:7. He said, "All ye shall be offended because of me this night: for it is written, 'I will smite the shepherd, and the sheep shall be scattered' " (Mark 14:27 KJV).

What Jesus said did happen. All the disciples, save one, scattered when Jesus was arrested. Only Peter followed the soldiers who had seized Jesus and eventually found himself outside the high priest's house while Jesus was on trial within. That scene played out like this:

Now Peter was sitting out in the courtyard, and a servant girl came to him. "You also were with Jesus of Galilee," she said. But he denied it before them all. "I don't know what you're talking about," he said. Then he went out to the gateway, where another girl saw him and said to the people there, "This fellow was with Jesus of Nazareth." He denied it again, with an oath: "I don't know the man!"

After a little while, those standing there went up to Peter and said, "Surely you are one of them, for your accent gives you away." Then he began to call down curses on himself and he swore to them, "I don't know the man!" Immediately a rooster crowed. Then Peter remembered the word Jesus had spoken: "Before the rooster crows, you will disown me three times." And he went outside and wept bitterly (Matthew 26:69–75 NIV).

Notice how those people knew Peter had been with Jesus. "Your accent gives you away," they said. Because Peter was born in Galilee, he naturally spoke like a Galilean. His identity was inborn, much like natives of Boston are easily recognizable by their speech.

Christians also have an inborn identity. We are born from above (John 3:3) and this new birth brings divine life into us. By birth we are marked as people of the kingdom of God. The more this life grows within us, the more we can be identified as believers in Christ. Just as Peter was recognizable because of his place of birth, likewise the divine life in us notifies others that we are Christ's followers.

Peter denied that he knew Christ, but because he looked and spoke like a Galilean he could never deny that he was born in Galilee. We who are Christian are recognizable, not by what we say, but by our birth. This we cannot deny. We are born of God and so the world recognizes us as children of God.

MEDITATION

But thanks be to God, who in Christ always leads us in triumphal procession, and through us spreads in every place the fragrance that comes from knowing him (2 Corinthians 2:14 NRSV).

IS IT RAINING, LITTLE FLOWER?

Is it raining, little flower?
Oh, be glad of rain!
Too much sun would wither thee;
Soon 'twill shine again.
Though the sky is black 'tis true,
Yet behind it shines the blue.

Art thou weary, tender heart?
Oh, be glad of pain;
Sweetest things in sorrow grow
As the flow'rs in rain.
God is watching, thou'lt have sun
When the clouds their work have done.

LUCY LARCOM (1824–1893)

This is what the LORD says. . . "They
have perverted justice by selling honest
people for silver and poor people for a pair
of sandals. They trample helpless people in

116

the dust and deny justice to those who are
oppressed" (Amos 2:6, 7 NLT).

Lucy Larcom, who was born in Beverly, Massachusetts, was the ninth of ten children. Her father died when she was very young and at age eleven she moved with her family to Lowell, Massachusetts, the nation's first planned industrial town. Because of an abundance of waterpower and a network of canals and railroads, Lowell was soon to become a major cotton-textile-manufacturing center. Larcom's mother became overseer of a female dormitory for a textile mill and Lucy herself worked in the Lowell mills for ten years.

The family arrived in Lowell at the moment when American industry began to significantly impact the world's economy. Troops of young girls like Lucy and her sisters were gathered from all around New England and Canada to work in the factories. Some of these girls were not more than ten years old, others were in mid-life, and the majority was between the ages of sixteen and twenty-five. Working hours extended from five in the morning until seven in the evening, with one half-hour each for breakfast and dinner.

It is interesting to place the sweet lyrics of this hymn against the hymn-writer's background in the Lowell mills where many a tender heart was weary and where, figuratively speaking, little flowers experienced constant rain.

Larcom provided a valuable account of the lives of these mill-girls in "Among Lowell Mill-Girls: A Reminiscence" (*Atlantic Monthly*, November, 1881). She also wrote of them in *A New England Girlhood* (1889) and in the long poetic narrative "An Idyll of Work" (1875). Although Larcom recalls millwork as tedious, her general tone is one of gratitude for the thoughtful planning of the mill owners.

True, Lowell was begun with the high-minded purpose of proving that the wretched working conditions in English factories were not a necessary by-product of industrialization. However, life at Lowell eventually changed.

Wages were lowered, the workload and hours were increased, and the living quarters deteriorated. One of the first labor strikes in this country took place in Lowell in 1836 when the mills announced that wages were to be cut. The strike failed. Larcom never expressed sympathy for those agitating for better pay and working conditions in the Lowell mills.

Her lack of sympathy notwithstanding, the gospel that Larcom believed gave rise to an awareness of justice that was previously unknown. It was not until the Bible was translated into the common languages of the people that effective agitation for social justice arose. Martyrs were made of the people who made this possible—English Bible translator William Tyndale (1494–1536) and the followers of the earlier reformer and translator John Wycliffe (c. 1330–1384). By making good use of the words of Scripture, reformers crafted convincing arguments against physical and economic oppression.

And so God chose things the world considers

foolish to shame those who think they are wise. Those who are powerless were able to shame those who are powerful (see 1 Corinthians 1:27, 28).

You don't have to look far to see that pioneering reformers were often Christian. Even those who did not profess the faith found inspiration among those who did. Among these reformers who heeded the potent Word of God were the following: Isabella Graham, who founded the Society for the Relief of Widows and Small Children in New York, 1790; Elizabeth Seton, who founded the first parochial school in the United States in 1809; Elizabeth Fry, who began the reform of English prisons in 1816; Catherine Booth and her husband William, who founded the Salvation Army; Dorothy Day, who founded the Catholic Worker movement in 1932; Rev. Antoinette Brown Blackwell, who pioneered the movement for women's suffrage; Amy Carmichael, who rescued girls from lives as Hindu temple prostitutes; Mary Dyer, who, while demanding religious tolerance, was hanged on Boston Common in 1660; and Harriet Beecher Stowe, who hastened the abolition of slavery with her book *Uncle Tom's Cabin*, published in 1851.

MEDITATION

"I hate all your show and pretense—the hypocrisy of your religious festivals and solemn assemblies. I will not accept your burnt offerings and grain offerings. I won't even notice all your choice peace offerings. Away with your hymns of praise! They are only noise to my ears. I will not listen to your music, no matter how lovely it is. Instead, I want to see a mighty flood of justice, a river of righteous living that will never run dry" (Amos 5:21–24 NLT).

It Is Finished!

Hark! the voice of love and mercy
    sounds aloud from Calvary;
See, it rends the rocks asunder,
    shakes the earth, and veils the sky:
"It is finished!" "It is finished!"
    hear the dying Savior cry.

"It is finished!" Oh, what pleasure
    do these charming words afford!
Heavenly blessings without measure
    flow to us from Christ, the Lord:
"It is finished!" "It is finished!"
    saints, the dying words record.

Finished all the types and shadows
    of the ceremonial law!
Finished all that God had promised;
    death and hell no more shall awe:
"It is finished!" "It is finished!"
    saints, from hence your comfort draw.

Tune your harps anew, ye seraphs,
    join to sing the pleasing theme;
All on earth and all in heaven
    join to praise Immanuel's name:
Hallelujah! Hallelujah!
    glory to the bleeding Lamb!

JONATHAN EVANS

I chose forty hymns for this book on the topic of comfort in trials, organized them alphabetically, and then began to write about them one by one. When this hymn came to the top of the list I asked myself, "Why did I pick this one? It's a hymn of praise." I went back to the hymnal and reread the lyrics. Only then did I realize that we encounter no more serious trial than the trial of our faith. Every suffering and temptation in some way tests our faith in God.

This is explicitly mentioned in Scripture by the apostle Peter: "Wherein ye greatly rejoice, though now for a season, if need be, ye are in heaviness through manifold temptations: That the trial of your faith, being much more precious than of gold that perisheth, though it be tried with fire, might be found unto praise and honour and glory at the appearing of Jesus Christ: Whom having not seen, ye love; in whom, though now ye see him not, yet believing, ye rejoice with joy unspeakable and full of glory: Receiving the end of your faith, even the salvation of your souls" (1 Peter 1:6–9 KJV).

Jonathan Evans has written this hymn of assurance, full of allusions to the word of God, to comfort anyone undergoing such a fiery trial.

It may seem obvious to say that the foundation of faith in God is the Bible. Still, in the midst of suffering, I can think of a dozen havens I turn to before seeking the Word of truth. How about you? The New Testament was written to give people like you and me full confidence and complete understanding of God's plan. This is centered in Christ himself in whom is hidden all the treasures of wisdom and knowledge.

When we have this understanding, no one and nothing will be able to persuade us otherwise. Recall the way you accepted Christ Jesus as your Lord. Now simply continue to live in him in the same way. Your roots grow down into him and draw up nourishment from him. And so you grow in faith, strong and vigorous in the truth, overflowing with thanksgiving for all the Lord has done.

When you are suffering it is easy to be drawn away by some philosophy or another. But philosophy is not Christ since in Christ the fullness of God lives in a human body. You are a complete person because of your union with him. This union is your refuge.

Once you were dead because of your sins and then God made you alive with Christ. He forgave all your sins. He canceled the record that contained the charges against you by nailing it to Christ's cross. In this way, God disarmed the evil rulers and authorities that tempt us away from Christ. He shamed them publicly by his victory over them on the cross of Christ (see Colossians 2:1–15).

So, dear believer, hear now the Savior's voice of love and mercy sounding aloud from

Calvary's cross: "It is finished!" "It is finished!" "It is finished!" "It is finished!"

PRAYER

Dearest God, here I am, listening to your voice of love and mercy that sounds from Calvary; that breaks the rocks, shakes the earth, and darkens the sky. Oh! Now I hear my dying Savior say, "It is finished!"

JESUS TRIUMPHANT

Jesus triumphant when the storm-clouds
    break,
And the loud thunder bids the soul awake;
When biting blasts lay earthly projects low,
And one by one the fondest treasures go.

Jesus triumphant, through the fleeting years;
Jesus triumphant, spite of blinding tears;
High over all, to hear thy loving voice,
Which bids the heart look upward and rejoice.

Jesus triumphant, when in work for thee,
Sad and disheartened, no results we see;
When gathered force of evil seems to win,
And work for Christ seems lost in work of sin.

Jesus triumphant all along the line;
Triumphant Savior, all thy triumph mine;
For since I am a partner in thy love,
My life on earth is lived through thee above.

Jesus triumphant when the spirit wings
Onward and upward to the King of kings;
And through the last great triumph of thy
*   grace*
Triumphant saints shall see thee face to face.

C. BUTLER STONEY

Jesus is triumphant, and I rejoice in this. Yet when the storm clouds of life break, they sometimes break on me. I've seen earthly projects laid low. And though I have few treasures, I've seen them go. Maybe you have, too. It's been awhile for me, but there have been days of blinding tears. In other words, though Jesus is triumphant, it seems that I am not. But this is just according to appearances. After all, "We live by faith, not by sight" (2 Corinthians 5:7 NIV). Or, as this hymn says, "Triumphant Savior, all thy triumph mine; / For since I am a partner in thy love, / My life on earth is lived through thee above."

Using the illustration of two kinds of bread, the sixth chapter of the Book of John shows the tension between living by faith or by sight. First Jesus fed five thousand people with five loaves and two fish. (vv. 1–15). The next day, in Capernaum, Jesus told some of these same people, "You only want to be with me because you ate your fill of bread yesterday. But you shouldn't be so concerned about perishable food. Instead, seek the bread of eternal life that I can give you. This is the reason God the Father sent me to you."

They replied, "All right, but what does God want us to do?"

Jesus told them, "This is what God wants you to do: Believe in the one he has sent" (see vv. 26–29).

"Fine," they said, changing the subject back to perishable food. "What miracle will you do for us? After all, the Scriptures say that Moses gave our ancestors bread from heaven to eat."

Jesus said, "No, Moses didn't give them that bread, my Father did. And now he offers you the true bread from heaven—the one who comes down from heaven and gives life to the world."

They thought he was talking about physical bread and that they would never be hungry again. So they begged, "Sir, give us that bread every day of our lives" (see vv. 30–34).

Jesus then had to speak even more plainly. "I am the bread of life," he said. "No one who comes to me will ever be hungry again and those who believe in me will never thirst.... For my Father has decided that the people who see me and believe in me will have eternal life— that I will raise them at the last day" (see vv. 35 and 40). The crowd was living by sight, thinking only of the perishable bread they hoped to eat. But Jesus, in these two sentences, explains how to live by faith.

You'll have to read this chapter for yourself to get all the details. In the end many of his disciples were offended at the idea that faith in Jesus Christ is the real food, the bread of life, and they deserted him. Realizing this, Jesus turned to the twelve disciples and asked, "Are you going to leave, too?"

May Peter's reply become everyone's answer

to this question. "Lord," he asked, "to whom can we go? Only you have the words that give eternal life" (see John 6:66–68).

Lord Jesus, I now by faith receive your triumph as my own. I am a partner in your love. So teach me, I pray, to live my life in you.

LIGHT AFTER DARKNESS, GAIN AFTER LOSS

Light after darkness, gain after loss,
Strength after weakness, crown after cross;
Sweet after bitter, hope after fears,
Home after wandering, praise after tears.

Sheaves after sowing, sun after rain,
Sight after mystery, peace after pain;
Joy after sorrow, calm after blast,
Rest after weariness, sweet rest at last.

Near after distant, gleam after gloom,
Love after loneliness, life after tomb;
After long agony, rapture of bliss,
Right was the pathway, leading to this.

FRANCES RIDLEY HAVERGAL (1836–1879)

Born in Worcestershire, England, Frances Ridley Havergal wrote many hymns that emphasize faith, devotion, and service to God.

The master of several languages, including Latin, Hebrew, Greek, French, and German, she was also a natural musician with a pleasing, well-trained voice and a brilliant hand at the piano.

This extraordinary woman was also a devoted Bible student who memorized large sections of Scripture. She practiced a disciplined prayer life and noted in her Bible the times and topics of her prayers. This is how she described her way of writing hymns: "Writing is praying with me, for I never seem to write even a verse by myself, and feel like a little child writing; you know, a child would look up at every sentence and say, 'And what shall I say next?' That is just what I do; I ask that at every line he would give me not merely thoughts and power, but also every word, even the very rhymes. Very often I have a most distinct and happy consciousness of direct answers."

She is called the "Consecration Poet" because her hymns often emphasize one's complete dedication to God. Significantly, her namesake was Nicholas Ridley, a prominent bishop who was martyred at Oxford in 1555. Although Frances Havergal died more than 120 years ago, her hymns are still loved and sung today. Other hymns by Havergal include "Who Is on the Lord's Side?" "Thou Art Coming, O My Savior," and "I Am Trusting Thee, Lord Jesus." A volume of her poetry titled *Poetical Works* was published in 1884. Her prose writings include *Kept for the Master's Use* and *Royal Commandments and Royal Bounty*.

Havergal's simple and wise hymn "Light after Darkness" is a reminder of the one thing that distinguishes the Christian faith from all religions and philosophies. That is the Resurrection. Each line of this hymn expresses the same idea in different words: Death is not the end. Havergal is saying what the apostle Paul said, though in a very different way. The apostle wrote, "So also is the resurrection of the dead. It is sown in corruption; it is raised in incorruption: It is sown in dishonour; it is raised in glory: it is sown in weakness; it is raised in power: It is sown a natural body; it is raised a spiritual body" (1 Corinthians 15:42–44 KJV).

In 1 Corinthians 15 Paul is not only talking about the resurrection of Jesus Christ. Above all he is talking about the resurrection of people who have died in faith. He writes, "For as in Adam all die, even so in Christ shall all be made alive. But every man in his own order: Christ the firstfruits; afterward they that are Christ's at his coming" (vv. 22, 23 KJV). Christ was resurrected from the dead. This is proof that all the dead will rise in the last day.

Certainly, the resurrection applies to our present lives as well. Havergal poetically lists many experiences that verify resurrection: light after darkness, home after wandering, sheaves after sowing, sun after rain, calm after blast, rest after weariness, near after distant, and so on. Although these are experienced by all people, not only Christians, our hope is not in these things. Rather, we look forward to the resurrection of the dead on the last day. Remember the apostle's advice: "If in this life only we have hope in Christ, we are of all men most miserable" (1 Corinthians 15:19 KJV).

MEDITATION

Joy cometh in the morning
(Psalm 30:5 KJV).

Another hymn by Frances Ridley Havergal is found on page 137.

LIKE A RIVER GLORIOUS

Like a river glorious is God's perfect peace,
Over all victorious in its bright increase;
Perfect, yet it floweth fuller every day,
Perfect, yet it groweth deeper all the way.

Stayed upon Jehovah,
Hearts are fully blest
Finding, as he promised,
Perfect peace and rest.

Hidden in the hollow of his blessed hand,
Never foe can follow, never traitor stand;
Not a surge of worry, not a shade of care,
Not a blast of hurry touch the spirit there.

Every joy or trial falleth from above,
Traced upon our dial by the Sun of Love;
We may trust him fully all for us to do.
They who trust him wholly find him wholly true.

FRANCES RIDLEY HAVERGAL (1836–1879)

"I will extend peace to her like a river, and the
wealth of nations like a flooding stream"
(Isaiah 66:12, NIV).

I used to sing this hymn with a slight change to the chorus, a change that made a big difference to me. Instead of singing the words, "Stayed upon Jehovah," I would sing, "Stayed upon Christ Jesus." While this still fit the metric pattern of the hymn's music, it also aptly fit my limited capacity for understanding God. Remember what the Scripture says: "No one has seen God at any time. The only begotten Son, who is in the bosom of the Father, He has declared Him" (John 1:18 NKJV). So, by considering Christ Jesus, we are at the same time setting our minds on God.

The first chapter of John explains this idea in another way. It begins with words that reverberate with eternal truth: "In the beginning was the Word, and the Word was with God, and the Word was God. . . . And the Word was made flesh, and dwelt among us. . .full of grace and truth" (John 1:1, 14 KJV). The flesh mentioned here is the man Jesus Christ. He is the Word who was God, lived with us, and discloses God to us.

This truth is also found in John 14. "If you know me," said Jesus, "you will know my Father also. From now on you do know him and have seen him" (v. 7 NRSV). Unfortunately then as now, there was some confusion about who Jesus is. Christ's disciple Philip spoke up, "Lord, show us the Father, and we will be satisfied" (v. 8 NRSV). Jesus was astonished. "Have I been with you all this time, Philip, and you still do not know me? Whoever has seen me has seen the Father" (v. 9 NRSV).

The New Testament gives highly detailed accounts of who and what Christ is. When you consider the words of Scripture, your mind is stayed upon Christ Jesus. The Bible overflows with potent passages like these:

Philippians 2:5–11 documents a hymn about Jesus that was sung by the ancient church; 1 Corinthians 13 describes Christ under another name—Love; Ephesians 1:3–14 tells of Jesus Christ by describing all the spiritual blessings that are ours in him; and Revelation 1–3 shows him as the resurrected and ascended Son of Man who is caring for the churches. In fact, the primary function of the New Testament is to reveal Christ. In this way it explains God and makes possible the promise of this hymn, "Stayed upon Jehovah, / Hearts are fully blest, / Finding, as he promised, / Perfect peace and rest."

MEDITATION

Christ is the visible image of the invisible God. He existed before God made anything at all and is supreme over all creation. Christ is the one through whom God created everything in heaven and earth. He made the things we can see and the things we can't see—kings, kingdoms, rulers, and authorities. Everything has been created through him and for him. He existed before everything else began, and he holds all creation together (Colossians 1:15–17 NLT).

Another hymn by Frances Ridley Havergal is found on page 132.

MY GRACE IS SUFFICIENT FOR THEE

I'll sing of the wonderful promise
That Jesus has given to me;
"My strength is made perfect in weakness,
My grace is sufficient for thee."
And lest my poor heart should forget it,
Or ever forgetful should be,
He still keeps repeating the promise,
My grace is sufficient for thee.

Yes, over and over and over,
My Savior keeps saying to me;
My strength is made perfect in weakness,
My grace is sufficient for thee.

His grace is sufficient to save me,
And cleanse me from guilt and from sin;
Sufficient to sanctify wholly,
And give me his Spirit within.
His grace is sufficient for trials,

No matter how hard they may be,
This promise stands over against them,
My grace is sufficient for thee.

His grace is sufficient for sickness,
Sustaining and making me whole;
His grace is sufficient when sorrows
Like billows roll over the soul.
His grace is sufficient for service,
It sets us from selfishness free,
And sends us to tell to the tried ones,
His grace is sufficient for thee.

His grace is sufficient to live by,
And should we be summoned to die
'Twill light up the valley of shadows,
And bear us away to him nigh.
Or when we shall stand in his vict'ry,
And Christ in his glory shall see,
We'll fall at his footstool confessing,
Thy grace was sufficient for me.

It is not our grace that's sufficient,

But his grace, it ever must be:
Our graces are transient and changing;
His grace is unfailing as he.
And so I am ever repeating
His wonderful promise to me,
"My strength is made perfect in weakness,
My grace is sufficient for thee."

A. B. SIMPSON (1843–1919)

This wonderful hymn by A. B. Simpson just about says it all about Paul's words on grace, found in 2 Corinthians 12:9. But there is much that can be said about the eloquent Simpson himself, one of the most respected figures in American evangelicalism.

Albert Benjamin Simpson was born on Prince Edward Island, Canada, and graduated from Knox College in Toronto in 1865. He accepted his first pastorate at Knox Church in Hamilton, Ontario—a large and influential congregation—and after eight years moved to the Chestnut Street Presbyterian Church in Louisville, Kentucky, where his health benefitted from the milder climate.

Simpson's physical weaknesses drove him to a deeper love for Jesus Christ and dependence upon God. He once told a coworker, "I am no good unless I can get alone with God." His practice was to quiet his spirit and literally cease to think. Then he could hear God's "still, small voice."

In Louisville, Simpson led a citywide revival during which hundreds of people were converted and received into the local churches. Soon Simpson had yielded himself to God in total surrender and from that point on he said he began to live "a consecrated, crucified, and Christ-devoted life."

From Louisville he went on to pastor New York's 13th Street Presbyterian Church. In 1881 he resigned this pastorate and began to hold independent evangelistic meetings in New York City. In 1897 he formed The Christian and Missionary Alliance.

Simpson's biographer A. W. Tozer writes, "For thirty years he continued to lead the society which he had formed, and never for the least division of a moment did he forget or permit the society to forget the purpose for which it was brought into being. . .'It is to hold up Jesus in his fullness, the same yesterday, and today, and forever!' "

About this Jesus, A. B. Simpson said:

> *I often hear people say, "I wish I could get hold of divine healing, but I cannot." Sometimes they say, "I have got it!" If I ask them, "What have you got?" the answer is sometimes, "I have got the blessing"; sometimes it is, "I have got the theory"; sometimes it is, "I have got the healing"; sometimes, "I have got the sanctification."*
>
> *But I thank God we have been taught that it is not the blessing, it is not the healing, it is not the sanctification, it is not the thing, it is not the it that you want, but it is something better. It is the Christ; it is himself. How often this idea comes out in his Word—"Himself took our infirmities*

and bare our sicknesses" (Isaiah 53:4).
"Himself bare our sins in his own body on
the tree" (1 Peter 2:24)! It is the person of
Jesus Christ we want. Plenty of people get
the idea and do not get anything out of it.
They get it into their head, and it into
their conscience, and it into their will; but
somehow they do not get him into their life
and spirit, because they have only that
which is the outward expression and sym-
bol of the spiritual reality.

I once saw a picture of the
Constitution of the United States very
skillfully engraved in copper plate. When
you looked at it closely it was nothing
more than a piece of writing, but when
you looked at it from a distance, it was the
face of George Washington. The face shone
out in the shading of the letters and I saw
the person, not the words, nor the ideas.
And I thought, "That is the way to look at
the Scriptures and understand the
thoughts of God, to see in them the face of

*love, shining through and through; not
ideas, nor doctrines, but Jesus himself as
the life and source and sustaining presence
of all our life."*

PRAYER

*Jesus Christ, I want to see your face, your
person, as I read the words of the Bible.
Save me from ideas and doctrines, and
give me yourself as my life and source and
sustaining presence.*

Other hymns by A. B. Simpson are found on pages 30 and 40.

Not Now,
but in the Coming Years

Not now, but in the coming years,
It may be in the better land,
We'll read the meaning of our tears,
And there, some time, we'll understand.

Then trust in God through all the days;
Fear not, for he doth hold thy hand;
Though dark thy way, still sing and praise,
Some time, some time we'll understand.

We'll catch the broken thread again,
And finish what we here began;
Heav'n will the mysteries explain,
And then, ah then, we'll understand.

We'll know why clouds instead of sun
Were over many a cherished plan;
Why song has ceased when scarce begun;
'Tis there, some time, we'll understand.

God knows the way, he holds the key,
He guides us with unerring hand;
Some time with tearless eyes we'll see;
Yes, there, up there, we'll understand.

MAXWELL N. CORNELIUS

One Old Testament prophet wrote, "The Lord God will wipe away tears from off all faces" (Isaiah 25:8 KJV). Certainly that time has not yet come because this hymn brings tears to my eyes. It mingles sadness with hope, just like in real life.

This life sees children lost, dreams dashed, and death arriving early. Most folks would agree that life is hard. Yet when it comes to hope, the Christian has the advantage, though our faith does not exempt us from life's distresses.

Consider the apostle Paul, chosen to explain God's plan. This honor got him into hot water when he was arrested with fearsome authority by the emperor Nero. Yet from prison Paul continued to tell of the plan, which God the

Creator of all things had kept secret from the beginning of recorded time. This eternal plan, carried out through Christ Jesus, is filled with hope, the hope that through the church God will show his rich and varied wisdom to all the rulers and authorities in the heavenly realms. How does this hope translate into daily life? It is simple: Because of Christ and our faith in him, we can now come fearlessly into God's presence, assured of a glad welcome (see Ephesians 3:9–12).

Maxwell Cornelius composed this hymn by rephrasing the famous words of Paul: "Now we see things imperfectly as in a poor mirror, but then we will see everything with perfect clarity. All that I know now is partial and incomplete, but then I will know everything completely, just as God knows me now" (1 Corinthians 13:12 NLT). Though Paul could only see dusky images of what the future held, he knew that what we suffer now is nothing compared to the glory God will give us later.

At the time of the fall of Adam, everything

on earth, together with the human race, was sub-jected to God's curse. Creation still groans under this curse and is looking forward to the day when it will be free from death and decay. Even though we Christians have the Holy Spirit within us as a small taste of that future glory, still we groan to be released from pain and suffering, waiting to receive our full rights as God's children. This includes the new bodies we have been promised (see 1 Corinthians 15:52–54).

A Christian's life is the ultimate in delayed gratification—we look forward to something incomprehensibly wonderful and we must wait patiently and confidently until it arrives (see Romans 8:18–25).

MEDITATION

Behold, the tabernacle of God is with men, and he will dwell with them, and they shall be his people, and God himself shall be with them, and be their God. And God shall wipe away all tears from their eyes; and there shall be no more death, neither sorrow, nor crying, neither shall there be any more pain: for the former things are passed away" (Revelation 21:3, 4 KJV).

NOT WHAT I AM, O LORD

Not what I am, O Lord, but what thou art;
That alone can be my soul's true rest;
Thy love, not mine, bids fear and doubt
    depart,
And stills the tempest of my tossing breast.

It is thy perfect love that casts out fear;
I know the voice that speaks the It is I,
And in these well-known words of
    heavenly cheer
I hear the joy that bids each sorrow fly.

Thy name is Love! I hear it from your cross;
Thy name is Love! I read it in your tomb:
All meaner love is perishable dross,
But this shall light me through time's thickest
    gloom.

It blesses now, and shall forever bless;
It saves me now, and shall forever save;

It holds me up in days of helplessness,
It bears me safely o'er each swelling wave.

'Tis what I know of thee, my Lord and God,
That fills my soul with peace, my lips with
     song;
Thou art my hearth, my joy, my staff, my rod;
Leaning on thee, in weakness I am strong.
More of thyself, O, show me, hour by hour;
More of thy glory, O my God and Lord;
More of thyself in all thy grace and power;
More of thy love and truth, incarnate Word.

HORATIUS BONAR (1808–1889)

Have you ever heard anyone say, "Why is God doing this to me?" Maybe you have said this yourself. Or, "What did I do to make this happen to me?" These are innocent, honest questions that are impossible to answer since they are not in sync with the truth of the Christian faith. A Christian relies entirely on who God is—and not at all on what he or she is. This gives the Christian faith its power.

The hymn-writer Horatius Bonar has provided a response to life's troubles that is faithful to the truth—"Not what I am, O Lord, but what thou art; that alone can be my soul's true rest." The first letter of John explains this: "And we have seen and testify that the Father has sent his Son to be the Savior of the world. If anyone acknowledges that Jesus is the Son of God, God lives in him and he in God. And so we know and rely on the love God has for us" (1 John 4:14–16 NIV).

While Scripture is so clear and so concise, here is a story that shows how muddy our thinking can be. I have a friend named Georgia, who is a Christian. When Georgia developed breast cancer that metastasized and spread into her bones, her only hope was a bone marrow transplant. Following this procedure, Georgia went all the way to death's door and then, by God's mercy, came back. While she was still in the hospital, Georgia received a letter from a Christian woman she had known in her former church. In short, this ill-timed missive explained why, in this woman's opinion, Georgia had gotten sick, had had a radical double mastectomy, and had nearly died and left her three sons motherless. The reason spelled out in the letter was that God was punishing Georgia for leaving that particular church.

Dear reader, if God were to punish us for the things we do, we'd all be dead. Furthermore, Christ's death would be meaningless. The woman who so freely condemned my friend Georgia didn't understand that "God showed his great love for us by sending Christ to die for us *while we were still sinners*" (Romans 5:8 NLT, italics supplied).

Every day let us remember that God is love. "Whoever lives in love lives in God, and God in him. . . . There is no fear in love. But perfect love drives out fear, because fear has to do with punishment. The one who fears is not made perfect in love (1 John 4:16–18 NIV).

PRAYER

*Oh, show me, hour by hour; more of your-
self, dear God. More of your glory, O my
God and Lord; more of yourself in all your
grace and power; more of your love and
truth, incarnate Word.*

PEACE, PERFECT PEACE

Peace, perfect peace, in this dark world of sin?
The blood of Jesus whispers peace within.

Peace, perfect peace, by thronging duties
    pressed?
To do the will of Jesus, this is rest.

Peace, perfect peace, with sorrows surging
    round?
On Jesus' bosom naught but calm is found.

Peace, perfect peace, with loved ones far away?
In Jesus' keeping we are safe, and they.

Peace, perfect peace, our future all unknown?
Jesus we know, and he is on the throne.

Peace, perfect peace, death shadowing us
    and ours?
Jesus has vanquished death and all its powers.

It is enough: earth's struggles soon shall cease,
And Jesus call us to heaven's perfect peace.
                    EDWARD HENRY BICKERSTETH, JR.
                                    (1825–1906)

You will keep in perfect peace him whose
mind is steadfast, because he trusts in you
(Isaiah 26:3 NIV).

It was 1875 and Edward Bickersteth, Jr., was vacationing in Harrogate, England, a popular health resort. The resort's sulfurous springs were believed to have such curative powers that even British royalty went to Harrogate to "take the waters."

While there Bickersteth heard a sermon on Isaiah 26:3, which reads, "Thou wilt keep him in perfect peace, whose mind is stayed on thee" (KJV). The minister pointed out that these words were originally written in Hebrew, the language of the ancient Jews, and that the Hebrew text does not actually say "perfect peace" but rather, "peace, peace." The repetition of the word peace, the minister said, indicates absolute perfection—"Thou wilt keep him in peace, peace. . . ."

Bickersteth was thinking about this later that day while visiting a relative who was sick and dying. Hoping to soothe the man's distress, Bickersteth read aloud from Isaiah 26:3. Next, he wrote these lyrics and read them to his kinsman. Notice that in his hymn, Bickersteth again and again repeats the soothing word *peace,* just like in the New Revised Standard Version translation of this verse: "Those of steadfast mind you keep in peace—in peace because they trust in you."

What one needs to enjoy this peace is a steadfast mind trusting God. But how can we have such a mind? The next verse helps with the answer: "Trust in the LORD forever, for in the LORD God you have an everlasting rock" (v. 4 NRSV). The trusting mind knows God to be the everlasting rock. This is not simply an understanding of this fact. It is solid knowledge gained from personal experience.

The apostle Peter had such an experience. One day Jesus told him, "Thou art Peter, and upon this rock I will build my church; and the gates of hell shall not prevail against it" (Matthew 16:18 KJV). While Peter came to *understand* that Christ is the rock, such a revelation was not what kept Peter in perfect peace.

Not long after this Peter came to *know* Christ the rock. This happened when Peter came to know himself. He had failed and denied that he knew the Lord (see Matthew 26:73–75). He gave up. He went away in tears. He lost his grip on all hope in himself and probably in everything else as well. He was left with nothing except Jesus Christ—and that was enough.

The day once came in my life when I let go of all hope—hope in myself, in God, and in other people. I was shaken loose and lost my grip because of bitter experiences with other Christians, people that I trusted and even loved. I began a spiritual freefall that lasted for many months. I lost my spirituality, my practice of prayer, and my friends in Christ. Finally, I spoke to God. "I don't care what happens to me," I said, "but you promised to accept me because of my faith in Jesus Christ and nothing more. I trust you for this. It is all I ask." With this prayer I landed on the everlasting rock of my salvation. And along with all the abrasions and bruises came peace, peace. Only then did I realize that throughout the years the core of my prayers, their fuel, was a desire for this personal knowledge of God's love and peace.

MEDITATION

Hear my cry, O God; attend unto my prayer. From the end of the earth will I cry unto thee, when my heart is overwhelmed: lead me to the rock that is higher than I (Psalm 61: 1, 2 KJV).

Precious Name

Take the name of Jesus with you,
Child of sorrow and of woe,
It will joy and comfort give you;
Take it then, where'er you go.

Precious name, O how sweet!
Hope of earth and joy of heav'n.
Precious name, O how sweet!
Hope of earth and joy of heav'n.

Take the name of Jesus ever,
As a shield from every snare;
If temptations round you gather,
Breathe that holy name in prayer.

O the precious name of Jesus!
How it thrills our souls with joy,
When his loving arms receive us,
And his songs our tongues employ!

At the name of Jesus bowing,
Falling prostrate at his feet,
King of kings in heaven we'll crown him,
When our journey is complete.

LYDIA ODELL BAXTER (1809–1874)

The tragedy of those who use the name Jesus Christ as an oath—spitting out the name in frustration or anger—is that for them the name has no meaning or power. Pity these people and pray for them. They have no idea of the indescribable marvel that is the name *Jesus*.

Clearly, Lydia Baxter knew the truth of this name. Though Baxter was an invalid for much of her life, she had a cheery, reassuring disposition. "I have a very special armor," she said. "I have the name of Jesus. When the tempter tries to make me blue or despondent, I mention the name of Jesus, and he can't get through to me anymore." Baxter's friends reported that they didn't visit her sickroom for the usual reasons. Instead of giving comfort and care, they themselves received encouragement at her bedside. Their blessing came because Baxter kept the two simple commandments of the New Testament: that we believe in the name of God's Son Jesus Christ, and that we love one another, as Christ commanded (see 1 John 3:23).

When you think about it, all names are important. They are shorthand for who a person is and what that person has done. For example, when you hear the name *Abraham Lincoln,* you think of the man who rose up from the American wilderness to become president and whose actions saved the Union. If you know the name *Emily Dickinson,* you think of a reclusive woman in a small New England town who wrote some of the best poetry in the English language.

But what is it about Jesus' name? If you know the name *Jesus Christ,* you know that "though he was God, he did not demand and cling to his rights as God. He made himself nothing; he took the humble position of a slave and appeared in human form. And in human form he obediently humbled himself even further by dying a criminal's death on a cross"

(Philippians 2:6–8 NLT).

In other words, this name declares that God became a human being and lived a perfect life among us. His death reconciled the entire creation to God. And because he was resurrected from the dead, Jesus stripped death of its power. Though many people have been presidents and many have been poets, not one has been or ever again will be what Jesus Christ is. "God raised him up to the heights of heaven and gave him a name that is above every other name, so that at the name of Jesus every knee will bow, in heaven and on earth and under the earth, and every tongue will confess that Jesus Christ is Lord, to the glory of God the Father" (vv. 9–11 NLT).

In the spiritual world, the word *Jesus* on the lips of a believer has power that cannot be exaggerated. Consider this: "Neither the sexually immoral nor idolaters nor adulterers nor male prostitutes nor homosexual offenders nor thieves nor the greedy nor drunkards nor slanderers nor swindlers will inherit the kingdom of God" (1 Corinthians 6:9, 10 NIV). But the Scripture doesn't stop there. "And that is what some of you were. But you were washed, you were sanctified, you were justified *in the name of the Lord Jesus Christ* and by the Spirit of our God" (v. 11 NIV, italics supplied).

MEDITATION

Let it be known to all of you and to all the people of Israel, that by the name of Jesus Christ the Nazarene, whom you crucified, whom God raised from the dead, by this name this man stands here before you in good health (Acts 4:10 NASB).

PRESSED OUT OF MEASURE

Pressed out of measure, pressed beyond all length;
Pressed so intensely, seeming beyond strength;
Pressed in the body, pressed within the soul,
Pressed in the mind till darksome surges roll.

God is my hope and God is my joy;
He is the resurrection life I enjoy.

Pressure by foes, and pressure from our friends;
Pressure on pressure, till life nearly ends;
Pressed into knowing none to help but God,
Pressed into loving both the staff and rod.

Pressed into liberty where nothing clings,
Pressed into faith for hard and hopeless things;
Pressed into life, a life in Christ the Lord,
Pressed into life, the life of Christ outpoured.

ANONYMOUS

Here in America, few people experience being

"pressed out of measure," a phrase taken from the King James Version of 2 Corinthians 1:8. When a severe illness strikes or a terrible accident occurs, pressure can ratchet up very quickly. The loss of income can do the same. But this hymn describes a level of pressure that is little known in this day and age.

From the beginning, the Christian tradition is one of suffering. When the people in the Greek city of Thessalonica received the message of the gospel, they had joy in the Holy Spirit despite their severe suffering. The apostle Paul wrote to them, "In this way, you imitated both us and the Lord" (1 Thessalonians 1:6 NLT).

Later, Paul gave the believers in Corinth a glimpse of what this suffering was like: "I think you ought to know, dear brothers and sisters, about the trouble we went through in the province of Asia. We were crushed and completely overwhelmed, and we thought we would never live through it. In fact, we expected to die. But as a result, we learned not to rely on ourselves, but on God who can raise the dead. And he did deliver us from mortal danger. And we are confident that he will continue to deliver us. He will rescue us because you are helping by praying for us. As a result, many will give thanks to God because so many people's prayers for our safety have been answered" (2 Corinthians 1:8–11 NLT).

The history of Paul's travels given in the Book of Acts tells something of what happened to the apostles in Asia. They first landed in Perga on what is now the southern coast of Turkey (Acts 13:13). Some scholars think that Paul contracted malaria in this low, swampy region. The chronic disease may be the thorn in the flesh he later complained of in 2 Corinthians 12:7. He was thrown out of Antioch of Pisidia (13:50), fled from being stoned in Iconium (14:5, 6), and in Lystra was stoned, dragged out of town, and left for dead (14:19). Returning to Antioch of Pisidia, Paul and the apostles strengthened the believers and encouraged them to continue in the faith with reminders that they must enter into the Kingdom of God through many tribulations (14:22).

Will this generation face such tribulations? Only the Lord knows. Thankfully, we have the example of the faith and patience of the inheritors of God's promises (see Hebrews 6:12), people like Paul and the other apostles. Paul said he worked harder, was put in jail more often, was whipped times without number, and faced death again and again. "Five different times the Jews gave me thirty-nine lashes. Three times I was beaten with rods. Once I was stoned. Three times I was shipwrecked. Once I spent a whole night and a day adrift at sea. I have traveled many weary miles. I have faced danger from flooded rivers and from robbers. I have faced danger from my own people, the Jews, as well as from the Gentiles. I have faced danger in the cities, in the deserts, and on the stormy seas. And I have faced danger from men who claim to be Christians but are not. I have lived with weariness and pain and sleepless nights. Often I have been hungry and thirsty and have gone without food. Often I have shivered with cold, without enough clothing to keep me warm" (2 Corinthians 11:24–28 NLT).

MEDITATION

All these sufferings and many more throughout twenty centuries have delivered the gospel into our hearts. If we pass through tribulation or not, may God teach us to sing with our spirits, "God is my hope and God is my joy; / He is the resurrection life I enjoy."

SAFE IN THE ARMS OF JESUS

Safe in the arms of Jesus, safe on his gentle
    breast,
There by his love o'ershaded, sweetly my
    soul shall rest.
Hark! 'tis the voice of angels, borne in a
    song to me.
Over the fields of glory, over the jasper sea.

Safe in the arms of Jesus, safe on his gentle
    breast
There by his love o'ershaded, sweetly my
    soul shall rest.

Safe in the arms of Jesus, safe from corrod-
    ing care,
Safe from the world's temptations, sin
    cannot harm me there.
Free from the blight of sorrow, free from
    my doubts and fears;

*Only a few more trials, only a few more
tears!*

*Jesus, my heart's dear refuge, Jesus has died
for me;*
*Firm on the Rock of Ages, ever my trust
shall be.*
*Here let me wait with patience, wait till
the night is over;*
*Wait till I see the morning break on the
golden shore.*

FANNY CROSBY (1820–1915)

If you want real comfort, take the idea of this hymn and go further, much further. Believers are not simply being held in Jesus' arms, but we are fully in Christ, living in him like we live in a house. This is a spectacular fact of the gospel's truth: When you believed, God put you into Christ. All who have been baptized, were baptized into Christ (Romans 6:3). Whether you were sprinkled or immersed, you are now submerged in Christ, completely covered by him.

When God looks at you, he only sees his beloved Son.

There are more verses in Scripture that illustrate this than can be mentioned in this space. If you conduct your own search, what you find will intensify your appreciation of your salvation. Use the following to begin your study of this truth, making sure to look up the references in the Bible.

The apostle Paul said that we live and move and have our being in God (Acts 17:28). His way of life was in Christ and he taught this in every church he visited (1 Corinthians 4:17). He spoke in Christ (2 Corinthians 2:17) and furthermore spoke the truth in Christ (Romans 9:1). Paul loved others in Christ (1 Corinthians 16:24), rejoiced in Christ (Philippians 3:1), and was imprisoned in Christ (Philippians 1:13). He had helpers in Christ (Romans 16:3, 9), and saw others in Christ (v. 7).

God's eternal purpose is in Christ (Ephesians 3:11) as are all of God's spiritual blessings (1:3). These blessings include the will of God

(1 Thessalonians 5:18), the love of God (Romans 8:39), redemption (3:24), sanctification (1 Corinthians 1:2, 30), righteousness and wisdom (v. 30), encouragement (Philippians 2:1), no condemnation (Romans 8:1), approval (16:10), perfection (Colossians 1:28), and triumph (2 Corinthians 2:14). Believers die in Christ (1 Corinthians 15:18) and will be made alive in him (v. 22).

Christ's believers are in Christ (Ephesians 1:1), the body of Christ is in Christ (Romans 12:5), and the church is in Christ (Galatians 1:22). God has "made known unto us the mystery of his will, according to his good pleasure. . .That in the dispensation of the fulness of times he might gather together in one *all things in Christ*, both which are in heaven, and which are on earth; even in him" (Ephesians 1:9–10 KJV, italics added).

PRAYER

Dear Father, your love that enfolds me
can never grow old or dim. In Christ

your love is centered and I am loved in
him. In him your love and glory find
their eternal rest; and in him your
believers are all so near and blessed.

(Adapted from a hymn by A. Carruthers.)

Another hymn by Fanny Crosby is found on page 25.

SOMETIMES A LIGHT SURPRISES THE CHRISTIAN WHILE HE SINGS

Sometimes a light surprises the Christian
    while he sings;
It is the Lord, who rises with healing in
    his wings:
When comforts are declining, he grants the
    soul again
A season of clear shining, to cheer it after rain.

In holy contemplation we sweetly then
    pursue
The theme of God's salvation, and find it
    ever new.
Set free from present sorrow, we cheerfully
    can say,
Let the unknown tomorrow bring with it
    what it may.

It can bring with it nothing, but he will
    bear us through;

*Who gives the lilies clothing will clothe his
    people, too;*
*Beneath the spreading heavens, no crea-
    ture but is fed;*
*And he who feeds the ravens will give his
    children bread.*

*Though vine nor fig tree neither their
    wonted fruit should bear,*
*Though all the field should wither, nor
    flocks nor herds be there;*
*Yet God the same abiding, his praise shall
    tune my voice,*
*For while in him confiding, I cannot but
    rejoice.*

WILLIAM COWPER (1731–1800)

The hymn-writer William Cowper was one of the most widely read English poets of the eighteenth century. Cowper (pronounced "Cooper") wrote of the joys and sorrows of everyday life with a concern for the poor and downtrodden. He described hedgerows, ditches, rivers, haystacks, and hares with a directness that was new to the poetry of his day. Because of this, critics consider him a forerunner of Robert Burns, William Wordsworth, and Samuel Taylor Coleridge, all of whom wrote in the nineteenth century.

Cowper was prolific. After his death his poetic work was collected into fifteen volumes. He is also considered one of the best letter writers in English. This is seen in his two-volume *Letters and Prose Writings*. Some of Cowper's hymns, such as "God Moves in a Mysterious Way" (collected in this book) and "Oh! For a Closer Walk with God," are staples of Protestant hymnody.

The son of an Anglican clergyman, Cowper lost his mother when he was six years old. As a young man he studied law in London, but after his father's death in 1756, the pressures of life precipitated his attempted suicide. During the eighteen months that he spent in an asylum, Cowper found faith in Christ. Later, he convalesced at Huntington in the household of

Reverend Morley Unwin. A pious Calvinist, Unwin supported the evangelical revival then sweeping English society.

When Unwin unexpectedly died in 1767, Cowper moved to Olney, Buckinghamshire. There he became friends with the Anglican curate, John Newton, a leader of the English revival. Newton encouraged Cowper in the faith and the poet's stay in Olney was characteristically productive. He collaborated with Newton on a book of religious verse, eventually published as *Olney Hymns* (1779). The best-known hymn in this volume is "Amazing Grace," attributed to Newton.

In 1773, however, Cowper relapsed into near madness. When he recovered the following year, he found his religious fervor had somewhat waned. After Newton departed for London in 1780, Cowper, having contributed many priceless gems to the church's hymnal, turned again to the vocation of poetry.

You see how a little knowledge of history can encourage your faith? The hymn "Sometimes a

Light Surprises the Christian While He Sings"
takes on a deeper, brighter meaning when sung
with the knowledge of who wrote it.

If you have ever suffered from slight de-
pression or sunk exhausted into the couch after a
difficult day, you know how dry the soul can
become when discouraged. William Cowper had
this experience in ways few people know. He is
certainly qualified to describe to the rest of us
his encounters with times "when comforts are
declining, when [God] grants the soul again a
season of clear shining, to cheer it after rain."

MEDITATION

Though the fig tree may not blossom,
Nor fruit be on the vines;
Though the labor of the olive may fail,
And the fields yield no food;
Though the flock may be cut off from the fold,
And there be no herd in the stalls—
Yet I will rejoice in the LORD,
I will joy in the God of my salvation.

The LORD God is my strength;
He will make my feet like deer's feet,
And He will make me walk on my high
hills (Habakkuk 3:17–19 NKJV).

Another hymn by William Cowper is found on page 74.

THE DAYS MAY YET GROW DARKER

The days may yet grow darker,
The nights more weary grow,
And Jesus may still tarry,
But this one thing I know:
The Lord will still grow dearer,
And fellowship will be
The closer and the sweeter
Between my Lord and me.

'Tis our dear Lord we wait for,
Our hope! Our joy! Our friend!
Himself we long to welcome,
And just beyond the bend
Hidden, perchance to meet us
Before the day is done,
The waiting will be over
And rest will have begun.

M. E. BARBER

Christ may return at any time and be waiting for us just beyond a bend in the road. This is a comforting thought, and it actually happened —on the very day of the Lord's resurrection!

On that day, as two of Jesus' followers were walking on the road to the village of Emmaus, Jesus himself came along, unrecognized by them, and began walking beside them. You might ask why these men were leaving Jerusalem on that day after such a momentous event. Maybe they had decided it was all over as far as Jesus was concerned and they had better get on with their lives.

The three men fell into a deep discussion as they walked along. When they arrived in Emmaus they sat down to a meal together. Only then, as Jesus shared a loaf of bread with them, did these disciples recognize him (see Luke 24:13–35). They had been with Jesus for months or even years. He had told them clearly that he would rise from the dead. But they weren't ready when he came after the resurrection.

The same thing occurred when Christ came

the first time. He was born into a world that was made through him, but the world did not recognize him. Even in his own land and among his own people, he was not accepted (see John 1:10, 11). The Jews had the unique God-given religion. For hundreds of years they had been praying and studying Scripture with all the prophecy about Christ. But they weren't ready for him when he came in incarnation.

And now it is our turn. As another beautiful hymn by M. E. Barber intones,

> *The church has waited long,*
> *   her absent Lord to see,*
> *And still in loneliness she waits,*
> *   a friendless stranger she.*
> *Age after age has gone,*
> *   sun after sun has set,*
> *And still in weeds of widowhood,*
> *   she weeps a mourner yet.*

Will we be ready for him? This question used to give me a shudder of fear. I found that despite all I could do to prepare my heart for the Lord's second coming, I never felt ready. In fact, the warnings to be prepared, and my attempts to heed them, made me focus more on myself and less on Christ.

One day this all came to a head. I was afraid that the Lord would come and I wouldn't be an overcomer (see Revelation 3:21). I walked out in my front yard and stood under the shade of an oak tree. As I looked up into the blue sky, I said, "Lord, I love you. I don't care what happens to me when you return. I only want you to come again and make this earth more wonderful than can be imagined." Suddenly my heart was freed from selfish worry.

So, what should we do while we wait? After all, he may be there just beyond the bend in the road. We should fight a good fight, finish the race, and remain faithful. And on the great day of his return, a prize awaits—the crown of righteousness that the Lord will give to all who have longed for his appearing (see 2 Timothy 4:7, 8).

MEDITATION

He who is the faithful witness to all these things says, "Yes, I am coming soon!" Amen! Come, Lord Jesus! (Revelation 22:20 NLT)

Another hymn by M. E. Barber is found on page 61.

THE GOD OF ALL COMFORT

I have been through the valley of sorrow
    and weeping,
The valley of trouble and pain;
But the "God of all comfort," the "God of
    all comfort,"
Was with me to hold and sustain.

As the earth needs the clouds and the rain
    with the sunshine,
Our souls need both sorrow and joy,
So he places us oft in the fire of affliction
The dross from the gold to destroy.

When he leads through the valleys of
    trouble and sorrow,
His mercy and love there we trace;
For the trials and sorrows he sends us
    in wisdom
Are part of his lessons in grace.

Yet how often we shrink from the purging
*   and pruning,*
Forgetting the husbandman knows
That the deeper and closer the cutting
*   and paring,*
The richer the cluster that grows.

O how well does he know that afflictions
*   are needed;*
He has a wise purpose in view,
And within the dark valley he whispers to
*   comfort,*
"Hereafter you'll know what I do."

As we travel the pathway thru life's
*   shadowed valleys,*
Fresh springs of his love ever rise;
And we learn that our troubles, our
*   sorrows, and losses,*
Are blessing just sent in disguise.

So we'll follow him faithfully where'er
*   he leadeth,*

The pathway be dreary or bright;
For we've proved that our God is the God
   of all comfort,
The God who gives songs in the night.
            From *Streams in the Desert,*
                        compiled by
            MRS. CHARLES E. COWMAN

Mrs. Charles E. Cowman was the wife of Rev. Charles Cowman, founder of the Oriental Missionary Society. The purpose of this organization was to evangelize and set up native ministries in Japan, Korea, China, and Formosa. Rev. and Mrs. Cowman served the Lord for twenty years until Rev. Cowman's failing health forced them to return to their home in California. While her husband was terminally ill, Mrs. Cowman compiled *Streams in the Desert,* a book of devotions with selections from various sermons, readings, writings, and poetry. At least nineteen editions of this book have brought encouragement to millions of people around the world.

Mrs. Cowman collected the poem "The God of All Comfort" from an unknown source and later it was set to music for the church's worship. It refers to 2 Corinthians 1:3–7: "Praise be to the God and Father of our Lord Jesus Christ, the Father of compassion and the God of all comfort, who comforts us in all our troubles, so that we can comfort those in any trouble with the comfort we ourselves have received from God. For just as the sufferings of Christ flow over into our lives, so also through Christ our comfort overflows. If we are distressed, it is for your comfort and salvation; if we are comforted, it is for your comfort, which produces in you patient endurance of the same sufferings we suffer. And our hope for you is firm, because we know that just as you share in our sufferings, so also you share in our comfort" (NIV).

The apostle Paul does not say how God comforted him in his troubles, but he does say that "the sufferings of Christ flow over into our lives." If the suffering is Christ's, it stands to reason that the comfort is also Christ's. Paul found himself in some extraordinary circumstances that brought him extreme suffering—so much so that he "despaired of life itself" (v. 8 NRSV). And although his sufferings were profound, yet were they ordinary. Indeed, they were the same things we suffer—sickness, pain, hunger, fear of death, sleeplessness, danger, and so on. Still, he calls these the sufferings of Christ.

What would the comfort of Christ be? Jesus Christ was a true human being like you and me, with one difference: He had no sin. Aside from his death on the cross, the things he suffered were the run-of-the-mill human sufferings, just like Paul's, and the comforts he experienced were the same as ours. Think of what comforts you. A cup of tea on a weary afternoon. Awakening to a clear sky and sunshine. A well-cooked meal, or even an ordinary meal prepared with love. An unexpected gift or favor. You make the list.

These are some of the comforts of the man

Christ Jesus. No, they are not supernatural or even spiritual, though we could add to the list of comforts the hope of eternal life and the joys of the New Jerusalem. Still, you see what I mean. These simple things come from the God of all comfort and this is why, when we receive them, we say, "Thank you, Lord."

MEDITATION

Therefore we were comforted in your comfort: yea, and exceedingly the more joyed we for the joy of Titus, because his spirit was refreshed by you all (2 Corinthians 7:13 KJV).

THE LORD WILL PROVIDE

Though troubles assail us and dangers affright,
Though friends should all fail us and foes all
  unite,
Yet one thing secures us, whatever betide,
The promise assures us, "The Lord will provide."

The birds, without garner or storehouse, are fed;
From them let us learn to trust God for our
  bread.
His saints what is fitting shall ne'er be denied
So long as 'tis written, "The Lord will provide."

When Satan assails us to stop up our path,
And courage all fails us, we triumph by faith.
He cannot take from us, though oft he has tried,
This heart cheering promise, "The Lord will
  provide."

He tells us we're weak, our hope is in vain,
The good that we seek we never shall obtain,

But when such suggestions our graces have tried,
This answers all questions, "The Lord will
    provide."

No strength of our own and no goodness we claim;
Yet, since we have known of the Savior's great
    name,
In this our strong tower for safety we hide:
The Lord is our power, "The Lord will provide."

When life sinks a pace and death is in view,
The word of His grace shall comfort us through,
Not fearing or doubting, with Christ on our side,
We hope to die shouting, "The Lord will provide."

JOHN NEWTON (1725–1807)

The old man Abraham and his only son, Isaac, were trekking up a mountain called Moriah. Abraham carried a knife and hot coals for a fire. Isaac carried a load of firewood. When they stopped to rest, Isaac said, "Father?"

"Yes, my son," Abraham replied.

"We have the wood and the fire," said the boy, "but where is the lamb for the sacrifice?"

Abraham answered, "My son, the Lord will provide a lamb" (see Genesis 22:5–8).

Three days before this God had told Abraham, "Take your son, your only son—yes, Isaac, whom you love so much—and go to the land of Moriah. Sacrifice him there as a burnt offering on one of the mountains, which I will point out to you" (v. 2 NLT).

This story illustrates why Abraham is called the father of faith. His poise in this incident portrays pure faith. Abraham truly believed God's promise that through his child Isaac he would inherit the earth (see Romans 4:13). His first faithful response to God's promise is recorded in Genesis 15:1–6. Understanding this, do you see Abraham's struggle in the dialogue with his son? If he were to kill Isaac as a burnt offering to God, the promise could never come true.

Isaac's question put his father in a most awkward place. If Abraham had said, "My son, you are the sacrifice," he would have been saying, "God's promise has failed." Instead, he responded with characteristic faith, "The Lord will provide a lamb."

The story continues. When Abraham and Isaac arrived at the place where God had told Abraham to go, Abraham built an altar and placed the wood on it. Then he tied Isaac up and laid him on the altar over the wood. Abraham took his knife and lifted it up to kill his son as a sacrifice to the Lord. At that moment the angel of the Lord shouted to him from heaven, "Abraham! Abraham!"

"Yes," he answered. "I'm listening."

"Lay down the knife," the angel said. "Do not hurt the boy in any way, for now I know that you truly reverence God. You have not even held back your beloved son from me."

Then Abraham turned and saw a ram caught by its horns in a thicket. So he took the ram and sacrificed it as a burnt offering on the altar in place of his son (vv. 9–13).

The six verses of John Newton's hymn "The

Lord Will Provide" depict many circumstances that may come into a believer's life at any time. When something happens to you, like Abraham you may say, "The Lord will provide." Remember what God provided to the father of faith and expect to receive the same.

Abraham looked up from the altar to which his son was tied and there, entangled by the horns in a thicket of brush, was a ram. This ram was all that was required for the fulfillment of the promise. This ram became the sacrifice.

The ram was strong and powerful. But the instruments of his power, his horns, were caught in a thicket. Isn't this ram much like Jesus Christ, the Son of God? In the act of becoming the man Jesus Christ, God became thoroughly entangled in the convoluted thicket of human existence. And God is still here in Christ as the Spirit.

When you declare and firmly expect "The Lord will provide," remember what was provided to Abraham in the most extreme trial of his faith—and expect nothing less.

MEDITATION

*It was by faith that Abraham offered
Isaac as a sacrifice when God was testing
him. Abraham, who had received God's
promises, was ready to sacrifice his only
son, Isaac, though God had promised him,
"Isaac is the son through whom your
descendants will be counted."Abraham
assumed that if Isaac died, God was able
to bring him back to life again. And in a
sense, Abraham did receive his son back
from the dead (Hebrews 11:17–19 NLT).*

Other hymns by John Newton are found on pages 35 and 45.

THE LORD WILL PROVIDE
IN SOME WAY OR OTHER

In some way or other the Lord will provide.
It may not be my way, it may not be thy way;
And yet in his own way, the Lord will provide.

Then we'll trust in the Lord, and he will provide;
Yes, we'll trust in the Lord, and he will provide.

At some time or other the Lord will provide:
It may not be my time, it may not be thy time;
And yet in his own time, the Lord will provide.

Despond then no longer; the Lord will provide.
And this be the token—no word he hath spoken
Was ever yet broken: the Lord will provide.

March on then right boldly: the sea shall divide;
The pathway made glorious, with shouting
    victorious,
We'll join in the chorus, the Lord will provide.

W. COOKE

His winnowing fork is in his hand, and
he will clear his threshing floor and will
gather his wheat into the granary; but the
chaff he will burn with unquenchable fire
(Matthew 3:12 NRSV).

Abraham was the first person with enough faith to say, "The Lord will provide" (Genesis 22:8). On the top of a mountain named Moriah, God provided a ram as a substitute sacrifice for Isaac. As it turned out, God had more in mind for that mountaintop.

In 1 Chronicles 21 we read that David's pride in taking a census of Israel set God's wrath on fire. Eventually the story comes to its climax at the threshing floor of Ornan. Ornan, a farmer, was a Jebusite, a descendant of one of the original inhabitants of the area now called Jerusalem. He and his four sons were peacefully threshing their grain, unaware that God was about to provide a sacrifice.

Threshing is the process of separating grain from chaff. The ideal place to do this is a hilltop where the breeze can blow the lighter chaff away from the grain. Not coincidentally, Ornan's threshing floor was on the top of Mount Moriah. While Ornan and his boys were working hard at threshing, they looked up and saw the angel of the Lord with a sword of judgment poised over Jerusalem. Then David and the elders of Israel appeared on the scene dressed in the sackcloth of mourning.

The story is one of the most exciting in the Old Testament. Ornan provided David with everything needed to make a sacrifice to God and thus, to stay the angel's hand of vengeance. His valuable threshing floor was the site, his threshing equipment was broken up for the fire, his wheat was the grain offering, and his oxen the burnt offering. Ornan had nothing left.

David gave Ornan six hundred pieces of gold in payment, built an altar on the threshing floor, and sacrificed burnt offerings and peace offerings. When David prayed, the Lord answered by sending fire from heaven to burn up the offering on the altar. Then the Lord spoke to the angel, who put the sword back into its sheath (see 21:25–27). David said, "This will be the location for the Temple of the LORD God and the place of the altar for Israel's burnt offerings!" (22:1 NLT). Later Solomon built the temple of the Lord on Mount Moriah "where the Lord had appeared to Solomon's father, King David. The Temple was built on the threshing floor of [Ornan] the Jebusite" (2 Chronicles 3:1 NLT).

All this happened on the same spot where Abraham revealed his faith in the words, "God himself will provide the Lamb," (see Genesis 22:8 NIV).

Threshing signifies judgment. John the Baptist said, "[God] will clear his threshing floor and will gather his wheat into the granary; but the chaff he will burn with unquenchable fire" (Matthew 3:12 NRSV). And like the ram provided to Abraham and Isaac, the sacrifices offered in the temple by the believing Jews were substitutes for themselves. God's righteousness was satisfied by these sacrifices and judgment upon sin was halted.

All these sacrifices foreshadowed the perfect sacrifice of Jesus Christ (Colossians 2:17; Hebrews 8:5; 10:1). The saying "God will provide" has much deeper significance than many people realize. It is simple for God to provide our material needs—look around at all you have and say a word of thanks. But this is not the point. Abraham's statement, "God will provide a sacrifice," prophetically pointed to the coming of Christ. He is what God has provided to us. When John the Baptist introduced him, he declared, "Behold! The Lamb of God who takes away the sin of the world!" (John 1:29 NKJV).

When you consider your life and think you have a need, maybe what you need is Christ. Then seize the promise and declare, "God will provide!"

MEDITATION

Christ is the head of the church, which is his body. He is the first of all who will rise from the dead, so he is first in everything. For God in all his fullness was pleased to live in Christ, and by him God reconciled everything to himself. He made peace with everything in heaven and on earth by means of his blood on the cross (Colossians 1:18–20 NLT).

Through All the Changing Scenes of Life

Through all the changing scenes of life,
In trouble and in joy,
The praises of my God shall still
My heart and tongue employ.

O magnify the Lord with me,
With me exalt his name;
When in distress to him I called,
He to my rescue came.

O make but trial of his love;
Experience will decide
How blest are they, and only they
Who in his truth confide.

Fear him, ye saints, and you will then
Have nothing else to fear;
Make you his service your delight;
Your wants shall be his care.

For God preserves the souls of those
Who on his truth depend;
To them and their posterity
His blessing shall descend.

NICHOLAS BRADY (1659–1726)

NAHUM TATE (1652–1715)

If you have been a Christian for awhile, this hymn's first verse could summon many thoughts of your life's history—all the changing scenes, the troubles and the joys. Think what has remained the same throughout the years. Your children have grown up and perhaps your parents have passed away. Likely you have changed jobs once or twice, which may have affected the state of your finances. How about your body or your health? Aging takes a toll on everyone. Friends have come and gone. The culture and the leaders of the government have changed and the natural environment may even have been altered.

Yet the praises of God still occupy your heart and tongue.

Don't be too hard on yourself. Certainly

there are times when one's heart seems cold toward the Lord. But these are only seasons of the heart, and the seasons change, too.

Think of all that has changed since this hymn was written. It dates back some three hundred years to the days when British and American churches were limited to singing metrical versions of the Psalms. Its authors, Nicholas Brady and Nahum Tate, wrote *A New Version of the Psalms of David* (1696)—the entire Book of Psalms rendered in rhyme and meter for use by choirs and churches. This was the Psalter of choice in English-speaking churches throughout the eighteenth century. Tate, who was the third poet laureate of England (1692–1715), was also a playwright who is best known for his adaptations of the Elizabethan playwrights. Brady was an Anglican clergyman, chaplain to King William II and Queen Anne, poet, and author whose work includes a blank-verse translation of Virgil's *Aeneid* (1726).

Isn't it easy to think that things were better

then than now? But this is not necessarily so. The world has utterly changed in three centuries. In some ways it is much better; and in others, so much worse. Yet the praises of God still occupy the human heart and tongue.

MEDITATION

Let brotherly love continue.

Be not forgetful to entertain strangers: for thereby some have entertained angels unawares. Remember them that are in bonds, as bound with them; and them which suffer adversity, as being yourselves also in the body. Marriage is honourable in all, and the bed undefiled: but whoremongers and adulterers God will judge.

Let your conversation be without covetousness; and be content with such things as ye have: for he hath said, "I will never leave thee, nor forsake thee.'" So that we may boldly say, "The Lord is my helper, and I will not fear what man shall do unto me."

Remember them which have the rule

over you, who have spoken unto you the word of God: whose faith follow, considering the end of their conversation. Jesus Christ the same yesterday, and today, and for ever (Hebrews 13:1–8 KJV).

'TIS NOW IN PART
I KNOW HIS GRACE

'Tis now in part I know his grace;
I catch sweet glimpses of his face,
But in that better world of his,
I shall behold him as he is.

Then shall I know as I am known,
And sing his praise before the throne;
Then shall I know as I am known,
And sing his praise before the throne.

'Tis now in part I know his love;
Bright sunbeams shine from skies above;
But glories more exceeding far,
Shall rise beyond life's evening star.

'Tis now in part I understand
The leading of my Father's hand;
But I shall own his ways were right,
When welcomed to his presence bright.

'Tis now in part, but O how sweet
To rest by faith at his dear feet;
Though now we see as through a glass,
The veil will lift, the shadows pass.

ANONYMOUS

"For now we see through a glass, darkly; but then face to face: now I know in part; but then shall I know even as also I am known" (1 Corinthians 13:12 KJV). So Paul describes the Christian's predicament.

Surely you have looked out a window at night when there is much more light within your house than there is without. The illumination on your face and on the room behind you makes reflections on the windowpane. These obscure the scene outside and the window becomes more like a mirror. This is what it is like to see through a glass darkly. Even the apostle Paul was vexed by his own reflection in the window of God's revelation. Though he understood the truth of the gospel better than anyone else, he only knew in part.

When Paul wrote, "We see through a glass, darkly," he was literally saying that the things of God are a riddle. The thirteen books of the New Testament that are attributed to Paul are his solution to this riddle, this puzzle. Yet he only knew in part. This is why "we walk by faith, not by sight" (2 Corinthians 5:7 KJV).

Sometimes you grope after God (see Acts 17:27), and sometimes you may have the strength to press yourself to seek God. As the apostle said, "Not that I have already obtained this or have already reached the goal; but I press on to make it my own, because Christ Jesus has made me his own" (Philippians 3:12 NRSV).

Paul was so determined that he considered everything worthless when compared with the value of knowing Christ. He claimed to have discarded everything (he called it all garbage) so that he could become one with Christ. He intensely desired to know Christ and experience God's resurrection power. He wanted to suffer with Christ, share in his death, and longed to experience the resurrection from the dead (see Philippians 3:7–11).

Still, Paul had to admit that he only saw in part.

When he faced his death he considered that his life had been poured out as an offering to God. "I have fought a good fight," he wrote. "I have finished the race, and I have remained faithful." And even though he only saw in part, Paul anticipated that the crown of righteousness would be given to him on the great day of Christ's return. Thankfully, the prize is not just for people like Paul who have the strength to press after the Lord, but for all who have long-ingly looked for the return of Christ (see 2 Timothy 4:6–8).

MEDITATION

Beloved, we are God's children now;
what we will be has not yet been
revealed. What we do know is this: when
he is revealed, we will be like him, for we
will see him as he is (1 John 3:2 NRSV).

WHAT GOD HATH PROMISED

God hath not promised skies always blue,
Flower-strewn pathways all our lives through;
God hath not promised sun without rain,
Joy without sorrow, peace without pain.

But God hath promised strength for the day,
Rest for the labor, light for the way,
Grace for the trials, help from above,
Unfailing sympathy, undying love.

God hath not promised we shall not know
Toil and temptation, trouble and woe;
He hath not told us we shall not bear
Many a burden, many a care.

God hath not promised smooth roads and wide,
Swift, easy travel, needing no guide;
Never a mountain rocky and steep,
Never a river turbid and deep.

ANNIE JOHNSON FLINT (1866–1932)

When I was fourteen years old some of my friends got motorbikes. These were low-powered motorcycles that, in Colorado, were legal for kids my age to drive. Naturally, I asked my dad to buy me one—an Italian Vespa or a Japanese Honda 50. I so much wanted one that I misunderstood my dad and thought he agreed to buy me one. But he didn't, and I was crushed when I learned the truth.

I think some Christians struggle because they don't really know what God has promised. They misunderstand the New Covenant and look for things that are not a part of the deal. Some of the things that God has not agreed to are listed in the verses of this hymn. But the chorus lists seven wonderful things that for certain God has promised:

Strength for the day—In Ephesians 3:16 Paul prayed for you and me and for every believer that out of the unlimited riches of God's glory the Holy Spirit will give each of us mighty inner strength. This does not mean that you will not sigh at the end of a hard day, weep over some great loss, be angry at some injustice, or in some way show your human weakness. Rather, it means that Christ will make his home in your heart little by little, day by day, as the Spirit does this strengthening work. In this way you are being rooted and grounded in love (see v. 17).

Rest for the labor—Jesus said, "Come to me, all of you who are weary and carry heavy burdens, and I will give you rest" (Matthew 11:28 NLT) These are heavy religious burdens—the exhausting labor of trying to be good. Here Christ speaks of the weariness caused by striving to be what you are not. After all, Jesus did say, "No one is good except God" (see Mark 10:18). Jesus Christ is the refuge from this vain trying. Remember, God made Christ, who never sinned, to be the offering for our sin, so that in him we can become the righteousness of God (see 2 Corinthians 5:21).

Light for the way—The apostle John spoke clearly: "This is the message he has given us to announce to you: God is light and there is no darkness in him at all" (1 John 1:5 NLT). John's guideline for knowing the light on the way needs no explanation: "Anyone who loves other Christians is living in the light.... Anyone who hates a Christian brother or sister is living and walking in darkness" (1 John 2:10, 11 NLT).

Grace for the trials—The apostle Paul received wonderful revelations from God, but he was also given a tormenting physical weakness. He called this a thorn in his flesh. Three different times he begged the Lord to take it away. The answer was the same each time: "My grace is all you need," said God. "My power works best in your weakness." So Paul began to boast about his weaknesses "so that the power of Christ may work through me." He became content with his weaknesses and with insults, his hardships, persecutions, and other calamities. "For when I am weak," he declared, "then

I am strong" (see 2 Corinthians 12:7–10).

Help from above—There is a word for this kind of help: *Incarnation.* This term is explained in the Gospel of John: "For God so loved the world that he gave his only Son, so that everyone who believes in him will not perish but have eternal life" (3:16 NLT). This is the ultimate and only help from above—the Word, who was God, became human and lived here on earth among us. He is the only Son of the Father, full of grace and truth (see John 1:14). Jesus Christ is our help from above.

Unfailing sympathy—If you have ever brought your troubles to a counselor or therapist, you know that although such people can be gifted, there is a limit to their sympathy. But we have a great high priest, Jesus Christ. He has passed through the heavens yet is able to sympathize with us. He understands our weaknesses because he faced all of the same temptations yet he did not sin. Go to the throne of grace, receive his mercy, and find grace to help when you need it (see Hebrews 4:14–16).

Undying love—Jesus loved those who followed him on his path through this world. When the time came to leave and return to his Father, he showed them the full extent of his love by dying for them (see John 13:1). Although Jesus died, his love did not. And now, because of his resurrection, we experience that love.

Another hymn by Annie Johnson Flint is found on page 89.

About the Author

Daniel Partner is an author and musician who lives in central Oregon. His recent books include *The Story of Jesus—A Portrait of Christ from the Gospels,* published by Barbour, as well as *Women of Sacred Song—Meditations on Hymns by Women* and *A Cloud of Witnesses—Readings on Fifty Women of Faith.*

Inspirational Library

Beautiful purse/pocket-size editions of Christian classics bound in flexible leatherette. These books make thoughtful gifts for everyone on your list, including yourself!

When I'm on My Knees   The highly popular collection of devotional thoughts on prayer, especially for women.
Flexible Leatherette. $4.97

The Bible Promise Book   Over 1,000 promises from God's Word arranged by topic. What does God promise about matters like: Anger, Illness, Jealousy, Love, Money, Old Age, and Mercy? Find out in this book!
Flexible Leatherette. $3.97

Daily Wisdom for Women   A daily devotional for women seeking biblical wisdom to apply to their lives. Scripture taken from the New American Standard Version of the Bible.
Flexible Leatherette. $4.97

My Daily Prayer Journal   Each page is dated and features a Scripture verse and ample room for you to record your thoughts, prayers, and praises. One page for each day of the year.
Flexible Leatherette. $4.97

Available wherever books are sold.
Or order from:

Barbour Publishing, Inc.
P.O. Box 719
Uhrichsville, OH 44683
http://www.barbourbooks.com

If you order by mail, add $2.00 to your order for shipping.
Prices are subject to change without notice.